Short, therefore, is a man's life, and narrow
is the corner of the earth wherein he dwells.

Marcus Aurelius Antonius, 121–180 AD

Believe in the Sign

By the same author:

LIFE AT THE TOP
(Queen Anne Press, 1998)

BLUE MOON
(Mainstream Publishing, 1999)

LIFE SENTENCE
(Parrs Wood Press, 2001)

Believe in the Sign

MARK HODKINSON

POMONA

A POMONA BOOK P-014
Mad in England!

Published by Pomona 2006

1 3 5 7 9 8 6 4 2

Pomona Books
PO Box 50, Hebden Bridge, West Yorkshire HX7 8WA, England, UK
Telephone 01422 846900 · e-mail ursula@pomonauk.co.uk
www.pomonauk.co.uk

Distribution: Central Books Ltd., 99 Wallis Road, London E9 5LN
Telephone 0845 458 9911 · Fax 0845 458 9912
e-mail orders@centralbooks.com · www.centralbooks.com

Reps: Troika, United House, North Road, London N7 9DP
Telephone 020 7619 0800

A CIP catalogue record for this book
is available from the British Library

ISBN-13: 978-1-904-59017-0
ISBN-10: 1-904-59017-9

Typeset in Granjon
by Christian Brett

Printed and bound in England by Cox & Wyman

The author wishes to thank the following for their help with this book: Paula Ridings, Roy and Jean Hodkinson, Ursula Lumb, Christian Brett, Richard Whitehead, Fred Eyre, Trevor Hoyle, Richard Lysons, Hunter Davies, Robert Kirby, David Luxton, Col Cavanagh, Kevin McCarra, Jack Hammill, Tom Palmer and the teams at Troika and Central Books. Several photos were kindly supplied by the *Rochdale Observer*. Thank you Chris Lloyd and Les Barlow. David James and Mark Wilbraham provided pictures too. The photo of Firgrove (courtesy of G. Wilson) and the Bread Roll Christ are from the Local Studies Collection, Touchstones, Rochdale. Dean Morgan supplied the copy of *Rap*.

NB: I have changed some of the names of people I mention but kept others if I felt they wouldn't mind being identified. Most of the stories are true, or near enough.

Finally, Rochdale AFC is a very different set-up today than the one I encountered back in the 1970s. I wouldn't want to put anyone off visiting a friendly and well-equipped club, especially since 2007 is our centenary year.

www.markhodkinson.com

CONTENTS

1. Death by Supermarket   1
2. The Quiet, the Fear   15
3. Everywhere but Nowhere to be Seen   28
4. The Sun Beat Down   45
5. Agoopa goopa goopa: Ha! Ha! Ha!   64
6. Petrol Blue Fading to Black   80
7. The Joy of Small Things   96
8. When Dreams Become Flesh   110
9. Not the Centre or Soul of the Party   130
10. Nudes in the Grass   147
11. Bread Roll Christ   161
12. On a Matter so Cataclysmic   178
13. A Chuckle in his Boots   188

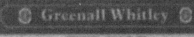

Greenall Whitley

THE DALE

ROCHDALE
WELCOME
TO SPOTLAND
A.F.C.

Crede Signo

(Believe in the sign,
Rochdale AFC's motto)

I

Death by Supermarket

BACK THEN MUMS AND DADS DIDN'T GO IN FOR quality time or anything so fey with their kids. They lived their lives (whatever that involved) and you were left to yours. You could play football in the street. Or lie flat on a railway sleeper floating through a culvert on the canal. Or you could follow the motorway for miles on the other side of the fence, passing through factory units and farm yards. Or you could see who could jump furthest down concrete steps on the stairwells at Ashfield Valley flats, carrying the whimpering victor home later. Or you could get out your bike and ride to Hollingworth Lake where the tougher kids, knees knocking, chins trembling, waded out into the icy blue, fearful of gigantic child-eating pikes.

Past the streets and houses there were places you could see; interesting, grassy places. We never got there, not properly. My mum and dad assumed the 'countryside' was private land with a farmer at every stile, gun in hand. Mum was usually cold too. We'd walk a few yards and she'd announce:

"It's bloody freezing. What are we doing out here?"

We'd run back to the car and pick at sandwiches wrapped in tin foil instead.

Dad was always knackered after work, covered in dust and aches and pains. He did a proper job which meant he needed a proper tea and a proper bath when he got back. By then it was nearly nine o'clock, time for bed unless *Sportsnight* was on.

I'm sure there were other family outings in the evenings but I can only remember two. The first was to see *Planet of the Apes* at the Odeon. The other was to Spotland, the home of Rochdale Association Football Club. We all went — dad, mum, my sister and me, on a Monday night in October 1974.

We sat in a shabby wooden stand full of middle-aged and old men, coughing and moaning. When Rochdale scored, they rose from their seats and patted each other on the back, smiling as if all was well with the world. The rain came down and the pitch and players disappeared in mist. We drank sweet milky coffee bought from a hut behind the stand. It had a low metal fence in front to direct the queuing but my sister and me ducked underneath because there was no one else around. The serving ladies lent on the counter tapping plastic spoons on the metal drums of hot water. Boxes containing Twix, Mars bars and Stimorol chewing gum were on the counter. The gum became slippy when you swilled coffee around your mouth while chewing.

"How are we doing? Still winning?" asked one of the ladies.

"No, they're drawing now."

"Usual story," she sighed.

Back in the stand, we stared through the wooden planks at our feet to the area beneath. It was piled high with discarded plastic cups, cigarette packets and sweet wrappers. A few minutes before the end of the game, the ladies from the tea bar shuffled down the shale track alongside the pitch carrying empty urns. They stopped and talked to people in the crowd.

The match ended in a draw. My mum and sister never went to Spotland again. Dad and me couldn't keep away.

Supermarkets had arrived in town and Tesco handed out car stickers to supporters at the game we attended. Asda, meanwhile, had moved into the disused Queens Mill in Castleton where it became known as the Asda Queens*.

Tesco was purpose-built with aisles as long as airport runways and girls working there who you'd last seen in a school uniform. They were now wearing pinafores with powder blue eye shadow and centre-parted hair.

The store held an opening 'party night' on the evening after the game with a promise of: 'Prizes, demonstrations

---

* I love the way these two words sound so dreamy when joined together. It suggests a beautiful place to shop but it wasn't, of course, being a draughty mill with ramps that went up and down like a fairground caterpillar.

and free sampling plus guest appearances by the star players.' We were supposed to be accompanied by an adult but even those that had come with their mum and dad were soon lost among the tins of beans and packets of frozen peas. Few of us recognised nor knew the names of the players so we mobbed any bloke looking too old to be at school but younger than our dads. When someone new was discovered in their nylon flared trousers, a gang of feather-cuts and snorkel parkas was soon upon them:

"Can we have your autograph, Mister?"

Afterwards the *Rochdale Observer* revealed that more than 2,000 kids had careered through the supermarket and the doors had to be closed intermittently to maintain order. I still have the programme containing the autographs. On the inside pages Hymie Showman of Yorkshire Street, Rochdale, advertises that he has won eight gold medals for his tailoring while Turner Brothers Asbestos has job vacancies in its sealing materials and reinforced plastics divisions. It offers 'secure employment' and complementary overalls —laundered free by the company. Rochdale AFC's Social Club is selling mild at 11p a pint, bitter and lager at 15p, and whisky and Cherry B at 13p a glass.

I didn't know Rochdale were one of the worst teams in the Football League. I soon bumped into its past. It was everywhere; drizzle soaking through your coat. They had spent all but five of their sixty-three years in the bottom division. My introduction to them coincided with their return back there. They had been relegated in ignominious fashion, winning two league games all season, conceding ninety-

four goals and finishing twenty-one points adrift of Port Vale, the club immediately above the relegation zone.

Moreover, the club had been effectively disowned by the town it purported to represent. The original spirit of co-operation that forged the club—and the town itself with the famous Rochdale Pioneers—had dissipated. They were seen as clinging vainly to a life made squalid by courtship with defeat and failure. They were mocked, their imminent demise anticipated with vengeful glee. Many felt they had dragged the town down for years, done nothing much apart from lose and whine about a shortage of money.

After one game I bought a bundle of old match programmes from the club shop. They smelled of damp. The pages were yellowing and the staples holding them together had rusted, bleeding dark orange into the paper. They covered a wide span of years, from the late 1940s. The editorials, year on year, were much the same: laments on defeats; appeals for more supporters; rhetoric that they would soon 'turn a corner' or 'find light at the end of the tunnel'. At least there was a poetical interlude. The advert for Leach's Pies of 163 Whitworth Road, Rochdale sang:

> 'Walk to the tea bar,
> straight as a die,
> count out your coppers,
> and ask for a pie.'

Krazy Kuts, Asda and Kwik Save were vying with Tesco for customers and the *Rochdale Observer* carried splashy adverts with girls in hot pants and banner headlines containing the words 'blockbuster', 'price busters' and 'once-in-a-lifetime'.

Tesco soon replaced Rochdale's 'stars' with an impressive and extensive list of allies. During its International Fortnight in-store guests included Stuart Damon of *The Champions*; *Coronation Street* actors Barbara Mullaney* (Rita Fairclough), Betty Driver (Betty Turner) and William Roach (Ken Barlow); the comedians, Frank Carson and Ken Dodd; and the *Dulux Dog*. The biggest attractions were 'the stars of *Planet of the Apes* in person', though parents were warned: 'In the interest of safety, children must be accompanied by parents when the apes are let loose in the store.' Krazy Kuts campaign was meagre in comparison. Its best offer: '99p summer tops'.

Tesco et al were bad news for Ronnie who owned the grocer's shop on the main road near our house. He had greasy, knotted hair and his jumper looked as if he'd poured the contents of a snow-shaker on it, such were the stains and dandruff. Ronnie's big love was his estate car, an eastern European make about as long as a railway carriage. When he parked it, he'd walk a few yards, stop, turn around and do this thing with his hands, making a rectangle with his thumbs and middle fingers as if imagining a frame around it.

I was working as a paper boy at the shop next door to his and Ronnie usually arrived as we were collecting the

---

* The actress later became better known by her married name, Barbara Knox. She is still in *Coronation Street* but her character name has changed also, to Rita Sullivan.

papers. He'd bank his car on to the pavement and start unloading. He only ever seemed to carry in tins of dog food, on cardboard trays shrink-wrapped in plastic. We'd all noticed this but Fenny, another paper boy, was the first to mention it:

"You must sell a lot of dog food, Ronnie."

"That's because there's a lot of bloody dogs around here, Brain of Britain!"

After that, Fenny barked when ever he saw Ronnie.

"Bugger off."

One morning Ronnie was struggling with heavy boxes when Fenny trailed him to the doorway and announced that his mum now shopped at Tesco.

"What does she want to do that for?" he asked, flabbergasted.

"She says it's cheaper and you can get everything in one go."

"Look, you remind your mam she gets a smile and a wink and a friendly welcome when she comes here, not like at some faceless bloody supermarket. Personal service, that's what it's called, personal service. You tell her."

He looked at Fenny as if he expected him to put down his bag of papers and run for home immediately with this vital message. When Ronnie disappeared into the rear of the shop, turning on the lights as he went, Fenny said to me:

"What's he on about, him? He never smiles. He's a right miserable bastard, he is."

My mum started going to Tesco as well. She went every Friday with dad and he normally hated shopping. It was as if they were going somewhere special like a show or a night-out. When they came back the first time they said how warm it was and well-lit. Girls dressed in funny costumes had offered them samples of cheese and foreign food from wooden tables. I asked if they'd had any. Dad pulled his face as if I'd asked him something absurd, like was it true mum used to be a trapeze artist.

"Not likely. It gives me indigestion that stuff. Your mam tried a bit."

If dad was working I went to matches on my own. I'd catch a bus to the town centre and board one of the football specials parked next to the war memorial. I took up position behind the goal at the Sandy Lane End, tight against the fence. I was usually in place an hour before kick-off.

We played Tranmere Rovers in the FA Cup. The crowd was 2,221, more than twice the size of the previous league match. As the ground filled up, the atmosphere was different than usual. People stood closer together, the talk was quicker and louder. The older lads at the back of the Sandy began singing just after 2pm:

"We all hate Scouse and Scouse and Scouse. We are the Scouser…haters."

The light was already leaving the sky soon after kick-off, rooftops and distant hills washed away in blackness. The world closed in to this patch of green upon which the ball was pummelled backwards and forwards. The volume increased when we won a corner and then dipped in anticipation as the ball was driven into the goal area. The shouting and swearing and singing sucked you in. I thought: this is what it probably feels like to be drunk.

Chants started and grew louder as more joined in. Who forged this noise? A face would be lit up briefly at the strike of a match, an image framed by bobble hats and scarves. Some songs trickled to nothing and their originator was mocked.

"Arrrrggh..."

While they jeered another chant broke out, loud and clear. They were united again:

"We are the Dale, we are the Dale, we are, we are, we are the Dale."

Afterwards we were disgorged on to the streets, exhilarated but the fellowship broken. We were each on our own to catch buses or walk home. The match was a draw. Tranmere won the replay. Dad told me later what a Scouser was.

Ronnie was doomed; death by supermarket. He usually replaced his car when the new number plates were introduced every August but he kept the same one that year. It was sagging at the back from all the tins he carried, the exhaust pipe inches from the tarmac.

He started to sell more beer than dog food and his shop became a kind of chemists, dishing out cans to the needy. Fenny said it was 'snooze booze'. He told me his dad called it this and that it got him through the day. Like many people in town he was between jobs—waiting for the mills to be flattened and replaced by trading estates. In a few years, instead of lugging bales of cotton, he'd be able to load coats and jumpers into wagons for Marks and Spencer or one of the other chain stores.

Among a team of toilers and bruisers, each looking as pale and ghostly as the other, Rochdale had a player of flesh and blood, meat and bone. Bob Mountford scored twice on his debut in January 1975 and was sent off in the next match after a scuffle with Chester's goalkeeper. He was tall and broad-shouldered with thick, curly black hair, a whitey with an afro: *six foot two; eyes are blue, big Bob Mountford's after you.*

His speciality was scoring from corners. The ball would be lobbed into the penalty area and Mountford careered recklessly through bodies to slam his forehead on to it. As he disappeared under a mob of joyous team-mates, they had to pick their way back to the half-way line through the debris of Mountford's barely legal challenge — shattered shinpads, ripped shirts, whining defenders, St John Ambulance men passing around the smelling salts. This was a brave man with a big heart. And big hair.

Word got around. Goalkeepers watched out for him when we were awarded a corner or a free-kick near their goal area. They knew what to expect but could do little to thwart it.

"Look, he's shitting himself," a fan would shout as we noticed their goalkeeper glancing nervously in Mountford's direction.

We enjoyed his fear and mocked his trepidation. It was sport at its crudest: two bodies set to collide, a test of strength and courage, you against him. The ball was incidental, something thrown down to legitimise the battle. Who had the most passion? Who was the bravest? We knew how much Mountford wanted it; we'd seen him week after week. The goalkeeper was aware of this reputa-

Bob Mountford: big hair, big heart.

tion and knew his adversary wouldn't flinch at a fist or elbow placed between him and the ball. Whether it was punched clear or hit the back of the net, the dual, a match within a match, lasted until the final whistle or until one of the protagonists retired hurt.

On my paper round I'd linger most mornings by the bridge over the canal and stare out across the water. It looked different so early in the morning: swamp-still with strips of wood, tyres, plastic bottles, shopping trolleys and traffic cones floating on top. In the gloomy half-light a few sparrows or starlings were the only signs of life. They picked at crumbs that broke off from discarded polystyrene tiles, mistaking them for bread. One time, vandals had thrown in a whole section of road works. The traffic lights switched from red to amber to green beneath the surface in ghostly blobs of colour.

The round started at Ashfield Valley, an estate made up of three-storey flats running alongside the canal. They were like something turned inside out and its guts put on show—corrugated edges, twisted metal, stones set in concrete. The disaffected were scooped up like cockroaches from all corners of town and let loose in the flats and on the landings: the unemployed, the sick, the single-mothers, the passing-through, the druggies, the dossers, the boozers, the thieves, the down on their luck. Tenants had to lie and say that they lived elsewhere to avoid the stigma of Ashfield Valley; stores refused credit otherwise.

There felt to be danger, even in the mornings. The lifts

The joyful Mrs Vera Hill, Ashfield Valley's first tenant.

stank of piss so I used the stairs instead. Walls were covered in graffiti, some of it about teachers at my school. On the stairwells between one floor and another were cartoon penises and messages: Julie is a slag, Paul is a tosser.

In every other block, loud music was being played with the windows open and the curtains torn down. Most weeks, someone fused. It was usually the quiet bloke you'd seen with his hood up walking defiantly from the shop back to his flat. The purposefulness of his walk gave him away. The landings were open but encased in metal cages so you could watch him disappear up the stairs or into the lift and reappear again, head bowed, marching towards his front door. Flats were often burnt out, a scorch mark running from black to watery orange upwards from the window. Police had taken him away. In a few hours the door would be forced and his stereo nicked.

2

The Quiet, The Fear

SPOTLAND WAS FALLING DOWN AROUND US. IT LOOKED old; not the pleasant 'old' of syrup-brown photographic nostalgia but a dank, murky, God-forsaken old. The stands, huts, dugouts and out-houses were like broken teeth, barely upright and left to decay. White paint had stained grey or flaked away like old skin. Damp had turned wood to the colour of cinder toffee and it crumbled to nothing in your hands. Rain seeped through the roofs.

At your feet, pressed up to the fences and retaining walls, were buckled plastic cups, jammed in among crisp packets and chip trays. The concrete flags on the terraces were cracked and uneven. The stumpy, uneven stands and much of the furnishings were like the final items at a remnants sale. Best offer accepted, make of them what you will.

In one corner, a raised section of the ground remained undeveloped and crush barriers had been forced down into soil and tufts of rough grass. Early in the season and just back from summer holidays, fans watched from 'the hill' and it was sometimes dry enough to sit upon. More often it was out of bounds, windswept and muddy, so we huddled in the stands, sidestepping puddles.

There had been stabs of glory—the solitary promotion and an appearance in the League Cup final of 1962 but principally it was a dogged pursuit of survival, a day-by-day, match-by-match grind of an existence. Out on the pitch, the players offered little beyond effort and fleeting glimpses of skill. Regular supporters griped that they could see better players on their local park. They still do.

I was about to take the stairs up a block of flats when I heard a noise from the bin store. I pushed open the metal door and there was a low sigh. I thought it was a cat or dog so I rattled the handle to scare it way.

I heard a voice.

"Hello," I said.

A ball of light appeared on the wall. I followed its trail to a torch. A boy of about my age was sitting up on a wooden pallet, a coat over most of his body and a stuffed carrier bag behind him for a pillow. His eyes were screwed up and he rubbed them. He shone the torch in my face and I held up my hand to deflect the light. I asked him what he was doing.

"I've just crashed here for the night. What time is it?"

"Just gone seven."

He had thin white arms and long tangled hair. The room reeked of rotting vegetables. I asked how he could stand the smell.

"You get used to it."

He yawned and pulled at his fingers. They made a cracking sound at the joints.

"What are you doing here?" I asked.

"I got chucked out last night by my mum's boyfriend. I just grabbed some stuff and legged it."

"Have you slept here all night?"

"I've tried to but it's bloody freezing."

I crouched down and the bag of newspapers touched the floor. He said he was hungry. I fished in my pocket and gave him what was left of a Toffee Crisp. I told him I called at the flats every morning and could bring more food if he wanted.

"Great," he said. "I'm going to be staying here a bit till everything's sorted out."

The next day I shoved a ham butty into my coat pocket and a small carton of milk. Dad had left the butty on the side, left over from his supper. I knocked quietly on the bin room door but there was no answer. The pallet was still there but the boy had gone.

At routine league matches the same few hundred people gathered in their usual meeting spots—a few yards to the left of the pie hut in the corner of the Sandy Lane End, others behind the goal or maybe under the Willbutts Lane stand, the 'scratching shed.'

It wasn't the same as being at a 'big' match where there was noise and passion and the enchantment of feeling insignificant, lost in the crowd. When supporters roared in the Kippax at Maine Road or the Stretford End at Old

Trafford*, you sensed your own smallness. All those voices joined together and created a sound that, for a few seconds, had a life of its own, ever-building and glorious.

The atmosphere at Rochdale was fractured. If five or six gathered together, perhaps mates from the same factory or pub, they could muster some camaraderie: a laugh, a chat, a piss-take, some shouting directed at the players. In the Sandy Lane End we tried to emulate the atmosphere of a big match and pressed together, jostling and singing. The songs and chants were usually quiet and half-hearted but supporters rallied and summoned a decent roar when a goal was scored. Even the older fans sang and the players responded. They looked across, almost as if surprised to find us there. They'd clench their fists or hold aloft a finger in salute.

Occasionally, maybe after a cluster of surprise wins or a cup match, the floating supporters returned. When the ground was fuller it became a place of rough charm and warmth. The extra faces and bodies were mortar between loose bricks.

Most nights, dad drank in a pub on the main road. We only went in once as a family, for a charity concert held one Sunday afternoon to raise money for a boy who had been scalded in the bath. They wanted to send him and his family to Blackpool. He was called Bobby but was known

---

* I had been taken to both grounds by my dad and grandad before we moved to Rochdale.

as 'Young Bobby' because, like a lot of people in Rochdale, he had the same name as his dad.

Almost everyone in there seemed to be smoking, the ash flicked into cherry-coloured metal ashtrays. Mum smoked Players No.6—I used to ask for them when I went to the Outdoor. She wafted the fumes from her face, chasing them from the pub's Formica-coated table with the back of her hand.

In the far corner under a black plastic sheet was an electric organ. Dad told us old Harold would probably play it before the show started properly. Dutifully, Harold rose from his seat and made his way across. He was unsure on his feet and it looked as if he might keel over before he reached the stool. Once he had his hands on the keys, he perked up. He flicked the ivory switches and proudly held back his shoulders as he pumped out patterns of whirring, liquid sound. He was joined a few minutes later by his pal, Tom. After one, two testing, Tom crooned that he'd left his heart in San Francisco and, then, that he wanted to be a part of it, New York, New York.

"The professional artistes will be along any minute now, ladies and gentlemen."

I knew from the start that a football ground was a place where it was more or less every man for himself. I was big-eyed, watching the match but also the people around me. In a few hours you might see enough to last a lifetime. You watched your back, checked where the exits were and ensured you were among enough of your own to repel an attack. Otherwise, the boot boys were coming to get you.

'Gatemen' in fawn coats supervised the opening and closing of gates around the ground. These were mainly old blokes, probably given free admission and a pie at half-time as payment. Visiting supporters were directed towards the Pearl Street End but there was no fence or wall to keep them in place. Police formed themselves into rough boundaries but they were easily breached, so home and away fans were constantly in the same parts of the ground.

Rochdale fans migrated at half-time to stand behind the goal they were attacking. We moved en-masse and away fans were corralled in the opposite direction around the pitch to swap places. The procedure relied on trust — that visiting fans didn't loiter in their original end or double-back and that Rochdale fans didn't lie in wait in our end, set to spring a surprise attack. Police sometimes mistakenly drove opposing sets of fans towards one another or formed a cordon across a walkway sealing off a handful from the main body of support, leaving them stranded and easy targets.

Dad knew the people gathering around the bar.

"They'll soon be bladdered," he said.

He was right. A few hours later they seemed to have doubled in size and volume. The room was suddenly full of shouters and bawlers, missing teeth, frown lines and beer-bellies, skinny women in short skirts, mad kids popping crisp bags, sly-eyed lads by the cigarette machine. Everywhere you looked, mouths were open, laughing or talking or shouting.

A few became reckless, screaming at one another and knocking over tables. My sister and me giggled as their punches missed and they padded around as if inside an invisible balloon. One couple reached an uneasy truce, holding each other up and shuffling around the tables. As they left, they nodded goodbyes and struggled to fathom the mechanism of opening the door.

Bert, another bloke dad knew, was sitting on a stool close to the bar, minding his own business. Dad said he was nice enough but could be a 'mithering old sod' at times. His hair was heavily lacquered and combed over to cover a bald spot. Dad said everyone knew he was as bald as a badger but it was up to him if he wanted to kid himself. Bert had a stutter. He had already come over to our table and said to mum that he didn't like these b-b-bloody concerts and all the noise and people acting like silly b-b-buggers.

At some games there was a sly and silent drift into our end as pockets of away supporters increased in numbers. Aside from their unfamiliar faces, they carried with them a look of cunning and daring, the affected sure-footedness of men on a mission. If you looked closely you could see their club lapel badges or a scarf tucked clumsily into a jacket pocket.

The air grew cold. We noticed the quiet, the fear. You could hear the shuffle of your feet against the cinders below, your heart beating. The game itself was spirited away. Players still harried and chased but it felt as if they were on the other side of a sheet of glass, drifting away. The score didn't matter: 3–0 win, 3–0 defeat, who cares now?

The older lads came alive on Saturdays. You'd see them at school not really up to much but when they marched through the Sandy to take up their positions they were kings of the world. On the bus back to town you'd overhear them. The week before they'd been on the coach to Hartlepool or Doncaster, they said. They'd chanted 'Up the Dale' in the bus station; fiddled money out of the cigarette machine in a pub close to the ground; got drunk, fallen over and been sick on a copper's shoes; intimidated passers-by; shown their backsides to people in cars driving past; pissed in a bucket and thrown it at each other. The shadows of their stories had lengthened through the week.

Alan, a mechanic who lived a few streets from us, was standing behind Bert at the bar. His shirt was undone to the third button and fastened to his body in saffron patches of sweat. The sleeves were rolled up. He had tattoos on his arms of naked women, anchors, playing cards and the red rose of Lancashire. He leaned over and dropped his hand on Bert's handiwork, his meticulously schemed hair.

"What's this, Bert? Fried, dried and slapped to the side?"

The men and women at Alan's table rocked with laughter. An overweight woman with a lowcut dress yelped loudest.

"Give over, will you?" said Bert, repositioning his hair.

"Come on, I'm only having a joke," pleaded Alan.

"There's some things you shouldn't joke about."

"Stop being so bloody miserable."

Alan raised his top lip to reveal a line of uneven teeth.

He altered his stance as if clenching the muscles in his shoulders and forearms. Bert was twenty years older than Alan and half his size. He made as if to smile, gulping and pushing his glasses up his nose. He didn't want any trouble, just leaving alone to have a drink, a smoke, a chat with his mates at the bar and back home for his Sunday dinner. All the same, he wasn't going just yet.

"I'll just have half, l-l-love," he said to the barmaid.

Alan was walking to his table with a pint in each hand, still staring back at Bert. The fat woman was frowning.

"You've bloody upset him now, you horrible bugger," she said. "Go and give him a kiss on his old bald head to make up."

"Nah, bugger him if he wants to take the huff."

She looked over at Bert.

"Oi."

He pretended not to hear.

"Just leave it, love," said Alan. "He's not worth a fart."

She puffed on her cigarette and scowled.

"I suppose you're right."

She looked down at her drink and then up again, staring towards the bar. She'd not finished yet.

"Old wanker."

The landlady heard and leaned over:

"Come on, no need for that."

"Tell *him* then," she said, pointing at Bert.

Bert took a final swig from his glass and climbed off the stool to leave.

Once or twice a season, the atmosphere was unbearable, horrible. You sensed the danger; you noticed it even on the walk to the ground. The chanting and threats from the other side of the pitch rang authentic. Their fans were at the fence. Voices had an edge. In skirmishes with police we could see that their movements were frantic. They hadn't come for the hollow artifice of running and chasing. These weren't the type to jab their instep into you half-heartedly when you fell to the ground. They'd even beat up kids and old blokes. So keep your mouth closed. Run anywhere you can to escape, on the pitch if necessary.

The etiquette of football hooliganism was peculiarly formal. First, the interlopers raised enough courage to announce their arrival. A deep, prolonged dirge of *Shaymen* might emanate from the back of the Sandy, for example. The Rochdale supporters, already aware of the incursion but not yet acknowledging it, turned and faced the gang of Halifax fans. Before they were attacked, these rival fans were sung to—in effect told they were about to be set upon. This was a crude courtesy allowing them time to withdraw. They had already strayed on to foreign ground, proved their mettle and could exit with a degree of honour. 'You're gonna get your fucking heads kicked in,' was the precursor, drowning out the Halifax fans, usually followed by: 'You're going home in a Rochdale ambulance.'

The final warning was the defiant, rhythmic chant of, "No one takes the Sandy." Thereafter, it invariably came down to weight of force. There was panicking and shouting and people falling over themselves to get away but ultimately the fight was over before it began, the smaller number acceding to the greater. During the fighting, the sound was noticeably different around the ground. People not embroiled in the 'aggro' fell silent, so the interaction between the terraces and what was happening on the pitch stopped. At the heart of this restless quiet were grunts, groans and the thud of bodies falling to the floor.

If the attack was resisted away supporters were marched from the home end by police. A ribbon of agitated youths — some in Doc Marten boots, skin-tight white trousers and donkey jackets, others in flares and parkas — filtered down the side of the pitch towards the Pearl Street End where the main body of visiting supporters was standing. They'd turn towards the home fans, flicking V-signs and shouting. The older Rochdale supporters barracked them as they passed:

"Bloody idiots. We've come to watch the football, not you lot. Bugger off home."

The old-boys condemned hooliganism but didn't want to see Rochdale supporters forcibly evicted from their own patch. They recognised the sanctity of the Sandy and that it formed the geographical epicentre of the club's support. It was a fundamental right to stand where you wanted and where you always had. Your dad might have stood there and your grandad before him and it didn't seem right that it should be occupied by a sneering, chanting mob from another town. They coveted this tiny, seemingly inconsequential piece of ground because they understood precisely that it defined a fiercely personal history.

Rochdale lost ten of their last eleven away games and went into the final match of 1974/75 against Swansea City at home needing a win to avoid applying for re-election.

The re-election system was often termed 'the trap-door'. Each season, the four clubs at the foot of Division Four were temporarily suspended from the League. The chairmen of the other eighty-eight clubs voted for them to be either reinstated or replaced by the country's best-performing non-League club. In practice the League was virtually a closed shop with very few clubs voted out. They had to perform consistently badly season after season for the pressure to become so great that the rest of the League could no longer uphold their membership. Even so, it formed a forbidding shadow because the consequence of losing League status, especially for a poorly supported club like Rochdale, was sometimes extinction.

When the rules of engagement broke down and fans were cornered or cut off from their mates, the consequences could be horrific. The gang would knock them to the ground and 'put the boot in.' Lads lined up and kicked at a body wedged motionless against a wall or fence. Between their blur of feet, you'd see an item of clothing or an expanse of flesh exposed under the onslaught. Older supporters pleaded mercy for these fallen kids. They were pushed aside, driven off by the pack. When the attackers were finally scared away by the oncoming police, they were victorious, laughing and embracing one another. The bloke who had tried to stop them earlier was now on his knees lifting the lad's head and cradling it in his arms, screaming after them:

"For God's sake, it's a football match, a fucking football match."

Swansea also needed a win on the last day because they were actually in the re-election zone with one point fewer than Rochdale. They brought hundreds to the game and the Sandy Lane End was a pit of unrest with charges and counter-charges. A large number of Swansea fans wore lab coats with 'Swan's Boot' written across the shoulders and a pair of studiously drawn Doc Martens underneath. I stood with dad close to the pie hut; this area always seemed better protected by police, probably to deter anyone from snatching the takings or, worse, burning it down.*

Rochdale won 1–0. Bob Mountford scored. We left before the end and could hear shouting and glass smashing behind us.

---

* This is not as outlandish as it might appear. Before the Bradford fire disaster it was fairly commonplace for fans to spark up their cigarette lighters maliciously. Rochdale flew a flag in the Pearl Street End for several seasons bearing the acronym 'RAFC'. During one game, visiting fans, from Blackburn I think, took it down and it was ceremonially burnt. It was never replaced although it hasn't stopped Rochdale fans singing their colour-modified version of the Communist anthem, *The Red Flag*.

3

Everywhere but Nowhere to be Seen

MY SCHOOL WAS HOPELESS. NO ONE DID ANY WORK. If they did they were viewed as a 'creep' or a 'homo'. Even the girls. While the teachers were fighting with the kids or staring out of the window wondering how they had ended up at this run-down school on a madhouse council estate I had plenty of time to daydream about Rochdale AFC.

I thought of them in the rain, training on the outskirts of the town centre close to the gasometer that looked like a giant industrial birthday cake. I imagined them jigging around cones, scurrying backwards and forwards over the wet cloying turf. They are wearing blue cotton tracksuits, the trousers tucked into white socks speckled with mud. Walter Joyce, the manager, is bellowing instructions, his anorak hood pulled over his head, his fingers plying the toggles. He encourages the players, retrieving balls that are fired high and wide.

After training they clamber aboard the mini-bus and head back to Spotland. They reach for towels in holdalls and scrub at their hair. The windows steam up and they make portholes with their shirt cuffs. Back at the ground they race from the bus, dodging puddles. They shower, don checked sports jackets and drive home in their Ford Capris and Vauxhall Vivas.

I imagined them on match days too, the clip-clipping sound of their studs reverberating around the changing room. Walter Joyce speaks to his players who are sitting on benches under metal pegs. Some stare down gravely, others fidget. Scraps of dried mud and grass are on the tiles. They tape on their shinpads, wrap laces around their boots and rub embrocation into their legs. A ball is bounced on the other side of the room, the sound sharp and tinny. Players are given instructions. They feign to pay attention but out there among the knees and elbows, boots and brawn, it will largely come down to instinct. As they leave, Joyce stands by the door and taps each of them on the back of the head:

"Good luck son."

The players run out to soft, reluctant applause. The air catches their breath, smacks their skin. The changing room is empty now, except for Joyce and Frank Campbell, the trainer. They impulsively shake each other's hands with great solemnity. They feel wrung out, emptied of emotion. They take one last look at the players' day clothes hanging from pegs and close the door quietly behind them.

I knew something strange had happened as soon as I opened the front door. The Fletchers, Steven and Philip, for the first time ever, actually looked like brothers. They stood very close together and appeared to have their arms around one another.

"Have you heard about Lesley?" said Steven.

I didn't know anyone called Lesley. They took turns to talk, one nodding while the other spoke.

"It's this little girl. They can't find her. They want people to help."

"I'll ask my mum if I can come."

My dinner had just been put out. I said I'd follow on later.

Lesley Molseed lived on an estate about a mile from our house. When news broke that she was missing, people stopped washing their cars and left their Sunday dinner on a low light. They gathered on street corners, forming search parties and retracing Lesley's route to the shop where she had gone on an errand for her mum. Kids combed wasteland, believing they stood a better chance of finding her because she was one of them. They knew the short cuts, the hidey-holes, the rickety wooden garages, the millponds and the mill yards, the abandoned cars, the tree-swings, the secreted piles of wood ready for bonfire night. They were sure they would find her lost in the long grass, sunk to her knees, cradling a doll, sobbing. It was an adventure: Christopher Robin had come to town and they were preparing trestle tables and cakes for the hero's party.

Tesco abandoned Rochdale AFC. The petrol vouchers, car stickers and autograph free-for-alls came to an end.

"We have not had one telephone call about our involvement with Rochdale FC," grumbled the store's manager to the *Rochdale Observer*.

The high point of my first full season as a fan, 1975/76, was a stirring win against Tranmere Rovers who were top of the league at the time. Rochdale were 3–0 up at half-time and serving up, according to the *Rochdale Observer*, a 'feast of footballing skills'. The game ended 4–1. I missed it. I was poorly on the settee, shivering under a pile of blankets.

The only teacher who ever showed much enthusiasm was Mr Day, and then only at certain times. He was our science teacher and overseer of *the* school video-player. He wheeled in this huge contraption every few weeks and asked that we fall into hushed reverence as he positioned it at the front of the class. By rights, he said (repeatedly), we had no author-ity to share room-space with this mechanical deity; it was usually exclusive to posh schools. At the end of the lesson he would ask us to remain seated so he could whisk it away without us knowing where it was stored. He was worried we might pass on information about its whereabouts to older brothers or friends keen to acquire it.

He had just two videos—one about plants showing their growth pattern speeded up and the other dedicated to anatomical oddities, many filmed in an eerie, fuzzy mono-chrome. He was unnaturally drawn to this film and it became a 'treat' if we did our homework on time or filed into the classroom quietly: any excuse would do.

"Shall we watch the freaks?" he'd sing.

"Yeah."

Flattened cardboard boxes were placed against the win-dows to blot out the sun and Mr Day cheerfully clunked down the huge buttons at the front of the recorder. The film began, the sound trembly, the picture scratchy. We saw babies covered in hair, people joined together, men with tails at the end of their spine, bearded ladies. The star was a pianist with eleven fingers. He played the piano joylessly as if it was his own death march.

Two days after the Tranmere match I was still wheezing and coughing and the colour of chicken soup. Rochdale had another home game; they often played on the Monday after a Saturday. By now the pilgrimage to Spotland was no longer a matter of choice for me and dad. We *had* to be there, sometimes together or separately if I went with my mates.

Dad made an appeal to mum on my behalf. I'd wrap up well. The fresh air would do me good. I was the 'other side' of my cold. He told her why it was so important: Rochdale had just won 4–1 and Northampton were next in line to get a bloody good hiding. He'd carry me there if necessary. Okay then, if you insist: he can go.

That night the biggest crowd of the season, 2,995, turned out to gorge themselves on another feast of football. We lost 2–0.

Before she went missing, Lesley, like most kids, was known only to a few people. The day afterwards her picture was in the papers and on television and we all got to know every-thing about her. She was eleven but looked much younger because she was barely four feet tall and weighed under four stones. She had been born with a heart condition and was susceptible to coughs and colds. On that Sunday she had been sent for a loaf and hairspray. When she was late back her mum became worried and began looking for her, shouting across garden fences to neighbours:

"Seen our Lesley?"

On the photo they released Lesley had a halo of curly black hair and a mischievous half-smile. Her eyes were dark brown with a watery sparkle as if she was about to burst out laughing. She was wearing tartan socks because she was a fan of the Bay City Rollers. Lesley was everywhere but nowhere to be seen.

Rochdale took eight matches to win again after their rout of Tranmere Rovers. The run included a 3–0 defeat at Brentford and three tedious 1–1 home draws. It was hard not to consider this as retribution for their audacity in outplaying a club heading for promotion. Since I hadn't actually witnessed the 4–1 win, this seemed doubly unfair. I had a lot to learn.

The kids on our street thought Alias Alias Face might have kidnapped Lesley. He was this tall lad we'd seen around with an unusually upright walk. The first time we saw him Steven Fletcher moved alongside and began walking the same way, looking across, smiling and showing off. Without speaking the lad grabbed Steven tightly by the throat. He was turning red. We shouted that he should let go. Philip ran to get their mum. Finally, he hurled Steven aside. While he spluttered, we ran after the lad.

"Why did you do that?"

"Because I did, didn't I?"

"He's coughing and everything."

"Deserves him right."

"He was only having a joke."

"He wasn't."

"He was."

"Well he's not laughing now, is he?"

"Where do you live?"

"Not telling."

"What's your name?"

"Not telling."

"Go on."

"Tony."

We saw him a few days later and he denied that he was called Tony. He said his name was David. After that we called him Alias Alias Face. We were convinced he had something to do with Lesley's disappearance.

Lesley's body was found. A joiner had parked his van in a lay-by on a moorland road over the border in Ripponden, West Yorkshire. At first he thought he had seen a pile of clothes but on drawing closer to the grassy ledge, realised it was a child's body. A blue linen bag with a crest of Tweety Pie was by her feet; her mum had given it to her to carry the shopping. She had been stabbed in the back, shoulders and head. Semen was found on her clothes.

MYSTERY PROWLER HINT IN MISSING GIRL SEARCH

I THINK SHE'S BEEN ABDUCTED—LESLEY'S MOTHER

FEARS were growing yesterday for the safety of 11-year-old Lesley Molseed, the 'hole-in-the-heart' operation girl, missing since Sunday lunchtime when she went an errand for her mother.

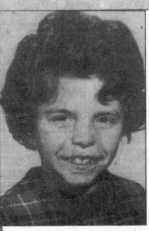

Mrs April Molseed, aged 38, thinks her daughter has been abducted. "I don't believe she is on Turf Hill. I don't believe she is in Rochdale," said Mrs Molseed in her council house "semi" at 11 Delamere Road, Turf Hill, yesterday. And Lesley's stepfather, Mr Daniel Molseed, a 40-year-old electrician, said: "She must have been abducted.

"We came to that conclusion on Sunday night when she did not come back. Everybody knows she is not a wanderer."

But Supt Bob Houghton, who is heading the massive police search operation, told the Observer: "We have no reason to believe that Lesley has been abducted, although all options are being kept open."

He said: "We are very concerned for Lesley's safety. We must be when there is no

LESLEY, who looks

35

Everything changed. We weren't allowed to play out any more. Mum walked with you to school, met you at the gates. Lesley's murderer was among us. The world became a cave, the light sucked out. He was beyond the fence at the bottom of the garden. He was in the back entry, flitting between the bins and boxes. He was by the railway sidings, bored, jabbing a knife into sleepers, marking time. He walked the park at night, a few steps behind the last boy or girl home, waiting.

It was hard to believe that we were so close to something that had been on the news every day. If you got on your bike, cycled down the main road and through a few back streets, you'd be at Lesley's house in about ten minutes. There, you could see for yourself where she had lived with her mum, dad, brothers and sisters. We thought: Lesley dying wasn't the same as if it had happened to one of us, was it? It couldn't possibly be chance, something that had happened indiscriminately. Life wasn't like that, surely. We imagined Jesus was waiting for her in heaven with everything she'd ever wanted. She was somewhere dreamy and beautiful, riding her bike, playing with a kitten, eating ice cream in the sunshine, waiting to be reunited with her family.

Going to matches set up unlikely associations. You had mates on the street, mates from school and others who accompanied you to football; maybe for one game or sometimes a whole season.

"Going on Saturday?"

"Aye."

"I'll come with you."

"Okay."

Gilly was a Rochdale fan but also supported Liverpool. He always had more stuff than the rest of us. He fancied himself as a goalkeeper and bought a pair of gloves with pimples on the palms similar to a table tennis bat. He wore a Liverpool tracksuit that was too small for him and pulled tightly across his chubby stomach. No one dared call him fatty.

He was the type of kid, who, if he went to the fair, claimed he had been on the Parachutes seventeen times or was one of seven lads who had 'shagged a girl' at the back of the Waltzers. He once said he'd broken into an office and pissed on the typewriters. Another time, he said he'd rubbed out the word *Anadin* from a tablet and sold it to a bloke in the park as heroin.

We'd meet at the bus stop on match days.

"Do you think there'll be any trouble today?" he'd ask.

"I don't know."

"I've heard they're bringing loads with them. You watch, it'll kick off. Bound to."

He often had this insider knowledge and had made plans:

"If I'm cornered, you know, if they charge into our end, do you know what I'm going to do? I'm going to get a cup of steaming hot coffee and I'm going to make sure the first one who comes near me gets the fucking lot in his face. I'll blind the bastard."

If he went to the toilets or for a pie (which he did a lot)

he routinely witnessed an act of violence.

"You should have been there then. Some Rochdale lads are beating up this Huddersfield fan. They're giving him a right hammering. His face is a fucking mess."

At other times he'd say a bloke had collapsed or an old lady's head had been 'split open' by a brick thrown from the Main Stand and there was a pool of blood at the bottom of the floodlight pylon. (I thought heads really did split open and that if I took the wrong turn out of the ground and passed an ambulance with its doors fastened back I'd see someone's head opened out like the covers of a book.)

Happy Christmas. The tension and fear that had fallen over the town ebbed away within a few hours on Christmas Eve, 1975. The streets and parks were safe again. We could play out.

Stefan Ivan Kiszko appeared before magistrates charged with the murder of Lesley Molseed. Eleven weeks had passed since the body was found. Kiszko was a big man; the papers all mentioned his size. The mums and dads on our street referred to him as a monster or a beast. I heard someone say he used to live on the other side of an iron curtain where there were forests, black lakes, ugly mis-shapen people and fog that never lifted.

Steven Fletcher said that Kiszko, honest to God, used to catch dogs, chop them up and boil them in pans. His moth-er had wanted a girl and dressed him in tights and skirts. He had no friends and was picked on at school. Fletcher said the house where he lived in Rochdale was old and falling down, surrounded by a high fence. Kiszko had taken out his rage and confusion with the world on a tiny child. People wanted to do to him what he had done to that girl. They wanted other prisoners to attack him, mutilate him, make him pay. My mum said he should hang. Frank, one of our neighbours, said hanging was too good for him.

Gilly's visions of sadistic violence were honed among the drizzle and darkness at Spotland. On my own with him on wintry afternoons and evenings, there seemed a flicker of truth in his stories. The recurring theme was of being trapped and out-numbered. When he became excited, his face flushed red as if licked by flames. When you left him, he felt to be on your skin.

He gradually gave up on football. He said he was too busy. He had to go into Manchester on Saturdays 'to see some lads from Moss Side'. At school he had developed a scam involving banana skins. He was collecting them, drying them on radiators in his bedroom, crushing them and selling the powder to kids who were told they would get high if they smoked it. Most knew the concoction had no effect but still paid up because they were scared of him.

Within days we knew all about Kiszko. The papers gorged on the story. He was twenty-four, single, lived with his mother and worked as a civil servant at the Inland Revenue. He was six feet, two inches tall and weighed more than eighteen stones. Six policemen flanked him in court.

Until a few weeks before his arrest the family home had been at the corner of a row of terraced houses close to an abattoir and a dairy, in the shadow of several mills. The windowsills teemed with dense, bushy plants and local kids called him 'Jungle Jim'. He was known because of his size, his waddling gait and his near-addiction to boiled sweets. If they pestered him long enough he would rummage in his pockets and chuck them a mint humbug or a pear drop.

One of Gilly's last matches was against Bradford City. Late in the game the referee awarded a corner to Rochdale. Bradford's full back gripped the goalpost while he waited for the ball to be sent over. He was black. His mouth was open and he struggled for air, drawing it back in deep gulps. His forehead was patterned with trickles of sweat that glowed under the floodlights. Supporters rushed to the edge of the pitch to shout abuse. Gilly looked about him:

"Watch this," he smirked.

Around us fans were booing and mimicking the squeals and grunts of monkeys. The player lifted his arm to mop away the sweat. When his arm fell to his side again, it seemed as if he had wiped away the previous expression. He was no longer lost to the game but apprehensive of the crowd. A man pushed his head between Gilly and me. He was as wide as three or four kids. I saw his face close up. The eyes were set apart. He had a large forehead. Spittle on his lips.

"Black bastard."

He was so desperate to say the words quickly that the

sentences broke down. They became barks of seething anger:

"Nigger. Cunt. Coon. Bastard."

The corner came over and the ball was cleared upfield. The players moved away from the goal area and the man turned to walk back up the terracing. It fell quiet again. Gilly had waited for the moment:

"My name is Kunte Kinte, I am *not* Chicken George," he shouted in a West Indian accent.

He had heard this on the television programme, *Roots*. Some of the grown-ups laughed and winked at him. Gilly puffed up, proud of himself.

Despite improving on the previous season and finishing 15th, Walter Joyce left Rochdale by 'mutual agreement' in May 1976. His footballing philosophy had produced entertaining matches but erratic results. We would win 4–2 one week, then lose 3–0 the next. He had doggedly sent out teams that adhered to the basic principles of what most fans considered to be 'good' football (which most subsequent Rochdale managers didn't): right footers were played on the right, left on the left; wingers were told to remain in the opponent's half, not chase back and cover as quasi-defenders; full backs were encouraged to overlap; young players were given their chance; and he liked the dynamic of big lad-little lad as twin strikers.

Alan, another mate from school, cycled to matches so he could save his bus fare for a tray of pie and peas at half time. I saw him before one match walking along the pavement outside Spotland, his trouser leg still tucked into his sock. I pointed with a rolled up programme.

"Bloody hell, I'm always forgetting ..."

After the game I walked with him to get his bike. He'd hidden it in bushes on wasteland a few streets away. It was getting dark. The banking fell away steeply to a wire fence around a factory, a hundred yards or so from a row of disused wooden garages. Rubbish was sitting in a shallow trough against the fence. The sun had bleached the colour from sweet wrappers and rain had washed away the patterns. He'd left it in the usual spot, leaning on its side among some dense rhododendrons. I heard him shuffle around, grabbing at branches.

"It's gone," he shouted. He thrashed about him with his feet. At first he did this to clear a space but his temper took over and he kicked out angrily. "Someone's nicked it."

I moved closer and stabbed at the ground with my heel, hoping to connect with metal and spokes.

"Did anyone see you put it here?"

"No. I always look around before I leave it. *Always*."

He'd built the bike himself. The frame was from a normal sports bike but he'd put cow horns on it and a springy leather seat.

"Shall we tell the police?"

He didn't want to bother. He wanted to go home.

"What's the point?" he said.

We walked back, lapping the ground before we saw two policemen striding across the club car park. We ran the last few yards and caught them up, breathless.

"You've not seen a lad on a bike, have you?"

The smaller one was putting on some gloves; it had become chilly.

"What kind of bike?"

I explained what it looked like.

"Why are you interested?"

I pointed at Alan.

"It's his. It's been nicked."

"Where from?"

"Over there, in some bushes."

"What was it doing in the bushes?"

"I always hide it there when I go to the football."

"Well you won't any more will you?" said the taller one.

"No."

Alan looked at me, bitter that I'd put him through this pointless ordeal.

We ambled home together. I said I'd help him find parts to build another. My dad was always in scrap yards where the skips overflowed with frames, handlebars, wheels and chains.

"You'll have another built in no time."

He shook his head. He hardly went to any matches afterwards

Within my first couple of seasons as a supporter I had identified a 'Rochdale' way of playing the game.* It was enterprising but gung-ho, bruising but honest. I seldom detected cynicism, either tactically or in spirit. If they did play blatantly for a draw or try to hold a lead they invariably messed it up magnificently. They soon resorted to type, charging upfield like kids let out at play time, attempting thirty yard cross field passes when a six-yard safety ball was more within their capability. This was the main attraction in fact: Rochdale's football was ambitious, the type that quick-steps with recklessness. I must have decided, probably on a largely sub-conscious level, that I liked that in my football clubs. And in people too. I blame Walter.

Stefan Kiszko, much like Lesley Molseed, had been a sickly child, plagued by asthma and blood disorders. At school he was let off PE because of poor health. He was extremely close to his mother (his father had died a few years earlier) and they were part of the community of Ukrainians, Poles and Hungarians that had come to work in the cotton mills after the Second World War.

The family had been doing well for themselves. A few weeks before his arrest, he and his mother had moved across town to live in a semi-detached house in a tree lined street. When the police called, Kiszko was sitting in his favourite armchair by the Christmas tree.

---

* This may not be true, however. How do any off us know what fastens us to a particular football club and keeps us there? I have arrived at this theory of 'the Rochdale way' by elimination really. If the ground was awful, the football dire and people were kicking hell out of one another on all sides, it must have been something intrinsic to the actual style of football. Possibly.

4

The Sun Beat Down

FEW BRITISH FOOTBALL CLUBS HAD COACHES IN 1976. Coaching was a modern concept, viewed as slightly effete and vainglorious. Most clubs had trainers whose role was fiercely non-scientific—a few press-ups, a run round the block, a slap of your bruised (possibly broken) ankle and a warning to go easy on the lager for a day or two.

Rochdale unexpectedly found themselves with the *Coach of the Year* as their new manager. His last job had been with the Australian national side. Much was made of his 'prestigious' award though no one had heard of it before.

The club was so proud of its new acquisition it hosted a buffet lunch before the season began and invited the press to meet him along with the players and directors.

Brian Green wore dark jackets and polo neck jumpers and, via the *Rochdale Observer*, was presented as the portal through which Rochdale would enter the modern age. He had travelled the world and returned to England overflowing with tactics, formations, training systems and diet plans. We had a visionary in the windowless office beneath the Main Stand.

He looked like a man who had enjoyed his time in the Australian sunshine. On his photograph in the paper he appeared loose-limbed and relaxed, light on his feet, a man with the belief that he could breathe life into the fading embers of a football club. I visualised him strolling on to the pitch, across the lush mid-summer grass and staring from one goal to the other. The groundsman is throwing him a wink and the *Rochdale Observer* taking his photograph, wishing him all the very best, Mr Green.

A football club, all of your own. Pass, pass, dribble, through-ball, wide to the winger, chip in to the centre-for-ward—goal! It must have seemed easy with the pitch uncluttered by bodies and the stands empty of know-alls and moaners.

Rochdale was sunny too, unusually so, in the summer of '76. Roads melted to black glue. It was eighty-two degrees in the shade and people were taken to hospital with sun-stroke. Firemen were called out 300 times one week, most-ly to grass fires, and police were allowed to remove their ties for the first time in the history of the local division. A reservoir on the moors was twenty-three feet below its normal level and the outline of the village on which it had been built was visible again. Water rationing was intro-duced and houses had supplies cut off for long spells.

We played out all summer. On some days it was so hot we flopped down on the grass, closed our eyes and watched the shapes and colours shifting across the underside of our eyelids. The area by the canal came alive with insects, chirruping and scratching. They jumped around your feet as you walked and each step felt to be detonating a small explosion. The grass grew longer than ever before, past belly buttons, so it was difficult to see the path snaking between the trees. The colours were brighter and deeper and the heat set the water sparkling.

A few of us found a railway sleeper and floated it down the canal. Steven Fletcher called it the *Good Ship Guzunder*. We took turns lying on it, tummy down, making our way through the tunnels underneath the road. These narrow waterways were lined with corrugated iron, so you had to press your body tight to the sleeper. In the middle it grew quite dark and sometimes you'd hear rats scurrying about. The circle of light at the end became bigger until you were out in the sunshine again, relieved.

Walter Joyce was the ghost of a winter departed. It hadn't been sunny then. He sent out his teams in wretched, clinging mud and they were rained on incessantly. Walter didn't have Green's joy de vivre. He was grey and stilted in his matchday suit, as if it had come back from the dry cleaners over-starched. He was Oldham-born, played for Burnley and Blackburn, parochial, prosaic, while a halo of light shimmered around Brian Green.

Rochdale appointed another sunshine boy to serve alongside him. He was a coach with, 'a reputation in Australian and New Zealand football which is second to none'. Alan Vest came to Rochdale via Gisborne City of New Zealand and the West Australian Federation FC. As a player he had captained New Zealand in qualifying matches for the 1974 World Cup.

Suddenly it appeared that we had the most cosmopolitan coaching staff in the Football League. Unknown to most people, Green had been born in Droylsden and Vest in Barnsley.

The sun beat down all summer. Dirt turned to dust. Footpaths dried and split into tiny fractures. Kids stripped off and jumped into streams and rivers to escape the heat. They formed parties and tripped through the streets with towels under their arms, dogs at their heels. We'd see them passing the end of our street.

"Where you lot going?"

They were heading to mill lodges or the quarries at Castleton, maybe Hollingworth Lake. We kept a distance, afraid that the dogs trailing them might have rabies. Adverts were on telly about the disease coming into Britain. Wardens drove around in vans on the look-out. They put a leaflet through our door: 'Stainless steel suits, a fleet of vans and an emergency information centre are included in Rochdale's plans to attack an outbreak of rabies.' If one licked us, even a little Jack Russell, we were told we could end up frothing at the mouth, spitting out saliva while the doctors injected us in the stomach with needles as big as your arm.

Green and Vest were framed for posterity in the match programme. Appropriately, page three was given over to a large photograph of them in casual attire. Both were wearing short-sleeved shirts with triangle collars. They were crouched on the Spotland turf, looking wistfully into each other's eyes. Vest's smooth-skinned arm rested on Green's knee. Their flared trousers were almost intertwined. Above, was the heading: 'Manager and Coach plan tactics.' Of course.

David Swann called round most days through the summer. He was tall and thin and whatever the weather wore the same baggy black duffel coat which had most of the toggles missing; he looked to have enough room to walk around inside it. The necks of his jumpers were either torn or stretched and his face was usually dirty; not soft dirt that could be wiped away with a dab of saliva on a handkerchief but pitted muck that needed a hard scrubbing to shift.

His dad had died a few years before and he was the oldest of three sisters and a brother. He had to sort these out and his mum who drank all day. This meant he became a kind of dad himself, though he was only thirteen.

Mum fed him. He wasn't used to proper dinners and teas and fell silent when he ate, collecting the food on his knife and fork meticulously. My sister had a few friends like this too who became part of the family for a few weeks or months.

Swanny was more open than other kids and enthusiastic. If he called and the plan was to build a den near the canal,

Manager and Coach plan tactics

he'd pull a piece of lined paper from his pocket circled in tea stains. He had included support props and bushes as camouflage, showing the exact location in relation to the road, flats and our house.

Steve Melledew, a player Rochdale had sold to Everton several years earlier, was Brian Green's first signing. When he left Rochdale he had a bowl haircut, lop-sided fringe and skin the colour of mashed potato. On his return the skin was much the same but he now had a feather-cut and, judging by the photographs in the paper, the self-assurance of a man who, like Green, had seen a world beyond the town's borders. In fact, the previous season he had played for Boston Minutemen in the North American Soccer League (NASL) alongside Eusebio.

During his earlier spell at Rochdale, Melledew's nickname had apparently been, 'the wild bull of the Pampas.' Not the catchiest of epithets.

In the holidays Swanny always called before nine o'clock. I wouldn't usually be up so dad gave him a cup of tea while he waited. It was as if he was so excited, he'd not been able to sleep. He told me later he had to get up early to dress and feed the rest of them. If his mum had been to the pub the night before she liked to lie in and he took up her tea and toast.

He was a member of the Scouts, the Boys' Brigade, church groups and some other clubs I'd not heard of before.

Steve Melledew. Form a queue, girls.

I went with him to Scouts. They met in a large room above some shops on a main road. About a dozen lads were kicking a football around haphazardly. It continually smacked against the windows, some of which were broken. Chairs were pressed up against the walls and long wooden canoes suspended in the roofspace across beams. At the far end, in an unlit area, was a pile of tents, Billycans, ropes and canvas bags.

A few kids wore fawn shirts but no one was wearing a full uniform. Swanny came closest but his shirt lap was hanging out and his trousers rode up past his ankles. A short, rotund man entered the room and bellowed that everyone should gather round. He was Skip, the leader. The group had two patrols, Cobra and Lapwing. I was told to stand in line with Lapwing and copy what the rest were doing.

The group was made up of lads I recognised from school. Some were from the roughest families in the area. Paul Jackson had been expelled after he set about someone with a bicycle chain. Skip told me I was allowed to wear normal clothes for a few weeks but I should save up to buy a uniform. Within three months I was expected to have the full gear. Afterwards some of the others told me they had been members for nearly a year and only had a shirt or neckerchief.

"Don't worry what Skip says. He's a dick."

On the way home a group of us called at the chippy and walked along eating our supper. When we'd finished we tossed the trays on to passing cars and held competitions to see who's stayed on the longest. After I'd been a Scout for a few weeks mum bought me a beret which was even better for hurling on to car bonnets.

Brian Green started the season with a squad of just fourteen players and this was pared down to eleven when three suffered injuries in pre-season friendlies. He drafted in an amateur player, Billy Boslem, to bolster the defence and they beat Scunthorpe United 1–0; it was their first opening day away win in thirteen years.

Season ticket prices for 1976/77 were £10 for adults and £5 for children.

Rochdale was uneasy in the sunshine, hot and bothered. The town was built to be rained upon or swathed in mist, joyous in a sulk. The heatwave broke the routine of indoor days and everything became warmed up and sore, played out in public.

We'd see drunks staggering home in the afternoon from one of the pubs where people sat at plastic tables outside the front door, breathing in exhaust fumes by the roadside. They were burned pink by the sunshine and usually angry about something, couldn't remember what. Some of the older kids baited them as they meandered by.

"Hey, you're pissed, you are."

They'd skip around, keeping a safe distance from flailing arms.

"Cheeky bleeders, come here."

The kids ran off laughing. The drunk would sit down, maybe on a garden wall, staring blankly at the traffic. Up on his feet again, he'd stop and fumble in his pockets, shifting his weight from foot to foot, blinking excessively and trying to stay awake. Each time he pulled a coin free from his pocket, he'd stroke it, scrutinising and raking out the muck and dust as if expecting to see his reflection.

The stifling heat was mentioned in the newspapers and on television during the Kiszko trial — the jury in shirtsleeves, barristers cooling off by wafting themselves with their papers.

My mum said she had heard that Kiszko had something wrong 'down below.' I asked what she meant.

"You know," she said and pointed to her crotch.

She was irritated by my puzzled expression.

"His *things* haven't grown properly. Can we leave it there, please?"

The court was told that a few weeks before his arrest, Kiszko had been admitted to hospital with anaemia. The doctors noticed he had a condition called hypogonadism; his penis and genitals were under-developed. He was given testosterone and the prosecution argued that a side-effect of these injections was sudden, uncontrollable sexual urges. For months afterwards, anyone at school showing signs of excitability was teased: 'What's up, are you on Kiszko pills or what?'

After hearing evidence for two weeks, the jury, on a 10–2 majority, found Kiszko guilty and he was given a life sentence. His former head teacher was asked for a quote. He said, curiously, that he was 'a very pleasant and often quite generous boy.' His hobbies and interests, listed

Stefan Kiszko with his mother, Charlotte.

assiduously in the papers, were stamp collecting, botany, photography, playing the accordion, attending the cinema with his mother, tending his father's grave and visiting garden centres.

The Brian Green effect appeared to be working. In their first sixteen games of the season Rochdale lost just twice and were close to the top four. Billy Boslem, despite looking like a 'new-born giraffe' according to some fans, had secured himself a professional contract.

"Let's talk of promotion," Brian Green told the press.

The Scout's summer camp was held in a wooded valley a few miles out of town. We couldn't put the tents up properly. Swanny tried to explain where the poles and guy-ropes had to be, but no one listened. Our pitching area backed on to a brook that tumbled through the valley. The noise and excitement grew as a new game developed—a series of inter-patrol raids. At first, one or two kitchen utensils were thrown in, but, as Swanny pleaded with them to stop, they worked their way up to food, sleeping bags and, eventually, a rucksack that bobbed up and down as it meandered downstream. The hubbub had alerted some nearby Venture Scouts. One raced over, concerned:

"What's going on? Has someone fallen in? How did that rucksack end up in there?"

"We just wuzzed it," said McCluskey.

"What for?"

"A laugh."

Other Scouts took off their shoes and socks and waded in to retrieve the stuff. They piled it in front of the tent that Swanny had finally put up. He thanked them excessively and tried to make light of the incident.

"Ah well, it needed a wash!"

Skip asked us to pool what was left of the food stocks to feed fourteen kids for three days: one jam roly-poly and a large tin of minced beef. We were fools to ourselves, he said. We'd let ourselves down, showed ourselves up. He suggested we ration it and try to last through the long weekend.

"Every time you get a rumble in your stomach it'll remind you what fools you've been, won't it?"

He left for a few minutes and returned to inform us that the camp had rallied and each group had donated two items of food each, which should be plenty.

Paul Jackson went missing soon afterwards. Skip told us at lights-out that the police had taken him from camp after he was caught threatening a *fellow scout* with a potato peeler.

Once or twice a season grandad would come with us to Spotland, mainly to give gran a break from looking after him. He hadn't been well for a good deal of his life. The illness was never properly classified but at various times was described as a 'breakdown' or 'premature senility.'

He was forgetful and confused, unless you got him talking about old footballers such as Frank Swift, Ted Sagar, Dixie Dean or Alex James. He could remember *everything* about them but didn't know whether it was Monday or Thursday or where the kitchen was in his own house.

He was always writing his name. He scrawled it on newspapers and scraps of paper. When I brought books home from school, mum had to keep them out of his way. He had spidery, close-together writing and never tired of scribbling his name. Gran said it was like a barometer. The harder he pressed down, the closer together the letters, the worse he was.

(Kiszko spent sixteen years in prison for a crime that forensic tests showed later he hadn't committed. The police, under immense pressure to find the killer, had effectively falsified evidence against him. He was routinely beaten in prison and, for his own safety, spent most of the time in solitary confinement. He suffered psychological problems, for a period refusing to wear clothes and smearing himself in excrement.

After he was freed, my dad drove past him once when he was carrying his shopping along Oldham Road. He said he shuffled as he walked and looked a 'broken man'. Kiszko died a year after being released and his mother soon afterwards. The man who killed Lesley has never been brought to justice.)*

---

* On November 5, 2006, Ronald Castree, aged 53, of Shaw, Oldham, was arrested and appeared two days later at Calder Magistrates Court, Halifax, charged with the murder of Lesley Molseed between the 7 and 9 October, 1975. He was remanded in custody.

Watford visited Spotland and their new chairman, Elton John, flew specially from Edinburgh to Manchester so he could attend. A few days before he had told *Rolling Stone* magazine — in an article picked up by newspapers throughout the world — that, 'there was nothing wrong with going to bed with somebody of your own sex.'

He was spotted in the directors' box and most of the Sandy Lane End moved en masse to the standing area in front of the Main Stand. They were a few feet beneath him, close enough to touch if they ran at the retaining wall and reached up.

Turning their back on the game for long periods, the fans sang incessantly: 'Elton John is a homosexual' and 'Elton John's bisexual army'. Kids raced to join the mob, not sure of what they were singing but lost in the mood of joyous mockery. It was like a party, everyone pointing and shouting at this squat, sorrowful figure in an overcoat in the semi-darkness above. The fans competed with one another:

"Hey Elton, think you'll come from *behind* and win this one?'

The other directors were warned:

"Watch out, he's got his eye on you."

Rochdale won 3–1.

Grandad went in through the same entrance as I did at Spotland, the one for kids and pensioners. At one match dad gave him the money to hand over and he dutifully fed it past the wire grille. The gateman pressed his foot on the pedal to release the turnstile. Grandad didn't move but stood upright with the metal contraption pressed against his thighs.

"Give it a push, pal," came a shout from behind.

He didn't know what to do and turned around slowly so he was facing away from the ground. The bloke leaned forward and forced the turnstile open with his hand so that grandad could get in.

"There you go. You've paid to watch this lot, no going back now."

During the matches he stared into space and couldn't involve himself in the game. Fans standing close by would speak to him:

"That was close, wasn't it?"

He'd nod his head.

We had to watch that he didn't wander off into the sparse crowd. When he went to the toilet dad shadowed him a few yards behind. I told him continually who our opponents were. He didn't ask but I felt he should know. The team in white was Darlington. Got that? Darlington. We're playing Darlington today, grandad—Darlington. He nodded.

"Who are we playing?"

"No idea."

When Rochdale scored he barely noticed. I would grab his jacket sleeve and tug hard with joy. People jumped all around, falling down the terracing.

"We've scored grandad, we've scored."

"Have we?"

The day after the raiding incidents we saw Skip laughing and joking while he was eating at the trestle tables in the leaders' canteen; he looked a different bloke away from us. He had to be fetched from there when McCluskey squirted lighter fuel into the mince. He claimed it would cook quicker if we set fire to the meat itself. Skip told us to boil it continually and scrape the oil from the top until it had all gone. We had about three grains of mince each for tea. They tasted of petrol.

After the camp I didn't play so much with Swanny. I started to anticipate him calling and tried to make sure I was out. Mum liked him but I had this idea that dad wanted me to mix with normal kids who played sport or at least went to school now and again.

I didn't see him until about a year later. He was at a bus stop. He had grown even taller, probably to more than six feet. His hair was really matted. He passed me a heavily creased card with his name and address on and a small photograph of himself.

"See that?" he said. "You've got a very valuable commodity in your hands. It's like a kind of passport. That card will get you anywhere within a thirty-mile radius for absolutely free. You can be in Cheshire in the morning and on the border with West Yorkshire by the afternoon. Brilliant."

He had qualified for this special bus pass under a scheme where certain kids spent time with companies for a few weeks before they left school a year or so later.

"I just tell them I'm on a mission, looking at the different towns where I might want to work when I leave school.

They don't check up on you or anything. I was at the air-port yesterday."

I asked what he'd done there.

"There's a viewing area. You can see the planes take off and land. I know some of the fellas. You know, the ones with the short-wave radios."

He said I could get a pass too if I whacked it off school for weeks on end and was put on the register. When I'd got one, we could travel to places together. He took a map and timetable out of his pocket.

"See here, it shows all the places of interest—historic halls, parks, things like that."

I asked him if he knew of anyone else he could pal up with if I didn't get a card.

"Not really. It doesn't bother me being on my own. I always have a good chat with the bus drivers. They let me stand at the front sometimes, right next to them. You can't beat it."

5

Agoopa goopa goopa: Ha! Ha! Ha!

ON THE DAY AFTER BONFIRE NIGHT, 1976, ROCHDALE took five coach-loads of fans to a match at Southport. A *Rochdale Observer* photographer was dispatched to record the clamour at Yelloways coach station. Almost everyone in the frame was giving the thumbs-up and had centre-parted hair and curtains of lank tresses down to their collar.

They waved silk scarves and had rosettes stuck to their lapels. One girl had placed two strategically on the front of her v-necked jumper. Another clutched a teddy bear. In the centre, a bushy-haired man with a Zapata moustache smiled grimly. Behind him was a woman in an overcoat with ruddy cheeks. She looked like she might have been on her way to Kwik Save, wandered over, and found herself in the middle of this crazy menagerie set for the heart of Southport.

Steven Fletcher invited us to take part in what he called 'an assignment'. He wanted to walk alongside the motorway heading in the direction of Manchester. We would follow the wooden fence as far as we could and climb over to walk on the other side, close to the hard shoulder, when we came to private land.

Only two of us volunteered—Steven's younger brother Philip, and me. We put fruit, chocolate and bottles of blue pop in plastic carrier bags and set off. We passed through fields where cows or sheep were grazing. When we reached farmyards and outbuildings we slipped over the fence to the motorway side. The banking was steep and tree-lined, so most of the time we weren't visible to passing cars.

The ground beneath our feet became marshy and my trainers turned brown up to the laces. After a mile or so we found some folders containing hospital records scattered on a piece of wasteland. We pulled out the X-ray photographs. Steven took one of a skull and another of a chest and jigged about as if he were a dancing skeleton, waving to the traffic below.

On the far left of the coach party was a brawny kid-bloke in extra wide flares, his hands shoved deep into the pockets of his heavily checked jacket. He had a silk scarf knotted tightly to his neck and draped over the front of his grandfather jumper. His sideburns were the size of sideboards and, unlike the rest of the party, he had poise. The rest were flotsam, happy to oblige and all pleased-to-meet-you but he was neither smiling nor waving. He stood perfectly still and serene as if aware of his importance, his cool. He was Moggy.

I wasn't on the photograph but it was my first away trip. While we waited for the coaches to arrive, I stood next to Andy Marcroft and his sister, Janet, who was about sixteen. She had made a large circular badge out of cardboard and stuck it on her stripy jacket. It read: 'Bob Mountford Eats Goalies'. A bloke passed and peered at it.

"You're right love, he does," he said before making his way to the back of the queue.

She could have smiled, nodded or carried on her conversation with Andy. Instead she turned and yelled to this retreating figure in full view of the other supporters:

"And he doesn't just have them for breakfast. He has them for dinner, tea and supper as well."

She said this with such gusto that some might have wondered what he had said to her. When she'd finished, she jerked her head forward as if finishing some vital business. Until this point in my life, I hadn't known what it was to cringe.

By late afternoon we were tired from all the walking. We'd dodged across connecting roads and through tunnels but kept losing sight of the motorway. The trees and hedges ended abruptly close to a large roundabout. We sat down on the grass in the shade of these last few saplings and watched the traffic. The sun had gone behind the clouds and the sky was the colour of a three-day old bruise.

Philip wandered off, stopping at a stile about fifty yards

away. He began kicking at some tall thistles. He snapped out with his feet, catching the thick stems half way along so the top part toppled over as if they had fainted. He was less successful with his karate kicks; he did these from the side, leaning away and pretending to shout out words in Japanese.

"Not bad, Bruce Lee," said Steven as we caught him up.

Steven ran at one thistle and booted it over the hedge.

"That's how you do it."

We kicked at them for a few minutes and a game developed where we had to decapitate the weeds of their fluffy heads with one clean kick. Philip won easily. He was wearing black leather shoes that were more effective than our trainers. Steven took up a stick and thrashed them to the ground. When he had finished we looked at the devastation. The broken stems were all around our feet, the fluff blowing across the field. Standing tall amid the destruction was one last remaining thistle. A breeze caused it to sway; it looked nervous in its solitude.

"Look at that cocky bastard," said Steven. "I'll show it."

He crouched and moved slowly, making a low humming sound. He shuffled his hands, mocking the spirituality of a king fu master, before jumping off the ground and slamming his foot into the stem. He ground the thistle down under his heel and placed the palms of his hands together, announcing magisterially:

"Let there be peace on earth."

I became aware of Moggy soon after I started supporting Rochdale. When he made his way through a turnstile, a whisper rippled across the ground: 'Moggy's here.' He had a distinctive walk, leaning forward on the pads of his feet, his hands raised as if about to start clapping.

His gang maintained a Saturday rendezvous on a small strip of terracing behind the goal. As he walked towards his domain, sometimes carrying a tray of pie and peas, he stretched his face fantastically and growled: 'Rochdale boys, we are here.' He looked mad, his eyes popping and his upper body shuddering with the effort. The spark of the chant ignited as his acolytes joined in loudly. He'd later bellow from the middle of the Sandy Lane End: 'Give me an arrrr-a-arrrrr,' as he ran through the spelling of 'Rochdale'. His voice was loud, deep and liquid.

During one season, he went missing. Word on the terraces was that he was subject to a court order and had to report to the police station at 3 pm on Saturdays. He couldn't resist Spotland and there was a fuss when he arrived at the turnstiles. Lads scrambled on to the banking inside the ground and looked down over the car park where Moggy was usually being led away by police officers. He went peaceably, almost as if he had sated the urge by merely walking in the direction of the ground and drawing close to it. At other times, he gained entrance. During a lull in play we'd hear his voice. He'd adapted a song to the tune of *Wandering Star*:

> 'I was born under the Sandy Lane
> I was born under the Sandy Lane

Knives are made for stabbing,
Guns are made to shoot,
If you're an Oldham fan
Then you'll get the fucking boot.'

He also sang a song that included the line: 'Agoopa goopa goopa: Ha! Ha! Ha!' Everyone laughed, even the police. After he had sung, these same officers moved into the crowd and Moggy was taken away. As he passed, supporters — many of whom didn't know him personally — bade him farewell. Some shouted over to annoy the police: 'See you next week, Moggy lad.'

We set off walking again. After a few minutes Philip began rubbing his stomach.

"What's up?" asked Steven.

"I think I need the toilet," he said.

"For a slash?"

"No."

"Well there's no bogs around here. You'll have to do it in a field."

"Have you got any paper I can borrow?"

I had a tissue stuffed in my pocket. I gave him that.

"Don't look, will you? Keep walking."

We said we'd carry on and he could catch us up when he had finished. He crouched in a hollow. He was still pleading as he took down his trousers.

"Please don't look. I'll catch you up in a minute."

Steven turned as if walking away but stopped in his

tracks. He waited a second before racing over, shouting. I jogged along behind. Without slowing, he lifted his foot and pressed the sole against Philip's shoulder, forcing him to fall backwards. Philip opened his legs as he toppled but his knees were fastened together by his underpants. He twisted and slumped awkwardly, landing face down. His bottom and the backs of his legs were white in the grass. He turned and lifted his head, reaching down to pull up his trousers. He was crying and shouting that his brother was a tightfuckingbastard.

Rochdale were drawn against the amateur side Northwich Victoria in the first round of the FA Cup. Brian Green announced confidently:

"There's no doubt we shall win."

The match at Spotland and the replay at Northwich ended in draws. The second replay was held at a neutral ground, Maine Road, home of Manchester City.

City were routinely watched by more than 40,000. The attendance at the cup-tie was 4,909. We were dotted around the ground randomly, lost in space. It was extremely cold. Dad and me stood at the top of the terracing, gripping a frozen crash barrier to save us from being blown out of the ground.

Occasionally someone from dad's local pub came with us to away games. This often coincided with a cup match or an upturn in form. We felt it dishonourable that they didn't support their hometown team on a full-time basis. It was as if we were suffering the club on their behalf—we had only moved to Rochdale a few months before our first visit to Spotland.

I always made a point of sitting in the front of the car; they weren't taking my place next to dad. We expected them, at the very least, to be circumspect with their opinions but they spoke as if *they* were the experts. If you listened for a while you could tell they had gleaned their information from the papers.

"They're not too good on their travels are they?"

"They won last week."

"Yeah, but that's the first in a while. They need to play more attacking don't they and the get the ball to the forwards a lot quicker?"

Dad would grunt a 'yeah' and this was, more or less, a signal that he didn't want to talk. The bloke in the back seat was left to stare out of the window. When we pulled in at a service station and our companion had wandered off to find the toilets or a sandwich, I'd question dad. I'd find out that he knew almost nothing about him.

"Has he got any kids?"

"I think so. Probably."

"Where does he live?"

"On Turf Hill, somewhere near St Joseph's."

"How come you know him?"

"I see him in the pub now and again, that's all. He's just someone I say hello to."

He'd only tolerate so much:

"What does it matter? Why are you asking all these

questions? He's just a bloke, that's all."

On the way back, if we had lost these interlopers were often more disgruntled than we were.

"They were crap weren't they?"

"Yeah."

"All the way up here to see that. It's a bloody disgrace. What do they earn at Rochdale?"

"I'm not sure, a few quid though."

"Bloody robbery. They've got a cheek even asking for wages. That full back, the blond-haired lad, he was useless. Absolutely useless. He'd have done more good sat in the stand with us, out of the bloody way."

We lost 2–1 after extra-time to Northwich Victoria, a team made up of plumbers and bricklayers who trained twice a week after work.

"We were humiliated," Green told the press afterwards.

Dad fell silent after the game and the hurt burned black around him as it did me. We were united in our disgust for those useless, heartless, hopeless bastards down there in the mist.

As we filed out dad said he wouldn't be buying the *Manchester Evening News* the next day as he normally did. I knew why: it would carry a lengthy report on the game, the Northwich players photographed with their arms around one another, spraying themselves with champagne next to the bath in the changing rooms, laughing and singing.

Rochdale fans left the ground with their heads bowed. I realised for the first time that football supporters were not a collection of individuals; they formed a collective heart.

That night, the heart ruptured. In the next three seasons we would twice finish bottom of the Football League.

Mum worked as a sewing machinist in a mill, making kids' clothes. She was leant over the machine all day running pieces of cloth under the needle. A couple of times a year she'd accidentally feed her finger through and it jabbed into flesh and bone. I'd persuade her to take off the plaster so I could see the purple and black under the nail. If it went septic she bathed it and kneaded pus from the wound.

Cheap imports led to the close-down of the textile industry in the 1970s. Round-the-clock working became a four-day week, to three, two, one, gone. Mum didn't like being out of work and took on jobs from home. She sold jewellery for a few months and had presentation boxes all over the house. She'd ask me if I liked the fleur-de-lis design best or the curved ones with blue stones set in them.

"Don't ask me!"

She organised parties at people's houses. In the brochure it said she could be a millionaire within ten years. She wasn't a saleswoman and neither were most of the other women taken on. They had nearly all been made redundant from the mills and were bored or feeling guilty being around the house while their husbands were at work and their children at school. They worked through their circle of friends, holding parties at each other's houses. They bought the jewellery (or Tupperware or Pippa Dee clothes) because they felt obligated. Most, including mum, did it for just a few months. They ran out of friends.

Trips away to watch Rochdale began to fall into a depressing routine. The journeys began cheerfully enough with dad checking the oil and water in the car; it felt a bit like going to the seaside.

We enjoyed being together. He wasn't one for small talk, so there were tracts of silence but it didn't matter. His mood changed if we were running late or unable to find the ground. He became agitated. He wasn't one for maps. He'd say 'we'll find it when we get there' or we'd arrive on the edge of a town and 'look for floodlights.' Minutes later we'd come to railway sidings or an industrial estate (which had their own floodlights) and dad, realising his mistake, would slam the car into reverse or swing it around recklessly.

Back on the main road, he'd slow down as we approached a pedestrian:

"Shall we ask him where the ground is?"

If I didn't answer quickly enough he'd drift past and grumble:

"I bet he would have known."

When we did stop and ask, dad leaned across, straining to hear. An old bloke, not quite sure whether we should take a left, right, or re-join the motorway, would lift up his cap and puff out earnestly:

"Now, let me think ..."

He had, at best, three seconds to think and if this wasn't enough, dad was off, accelerating away. It was as if the match was a matter of life and death. Dad even acknowledged this himself, sitting back in his chair, momentarily giving up:

"It's not a matter of life and death, is it?"

If, at that instant, he saw what he thought was football traffic backing up at the next set of lights, he was drawn back to his battle between the clock and hope. He'd jab hard at the accelerator, zipping down a back street.

"Come on, we might just make it."

We usually arrived five minutes after kick-off but were once so late at Tranmere Rovers that we had to bang on the turnstile doors to get in. It was almost half-time and they let us in for free.

I came home from school earlier than expected one afternoon. Mum wasn't pleased to see me.

"What are you doing here now?" she snapped.

"The teacher's off ill, so we've been let off last lesson."

"Come in."

I walked through the living room into the kitchen. Boxes were piled high on the table. I could smell burning.

"What's this?" I asked.

"My new job."

"What is it?"

"Don't be so nosy. I didn't want you to find out."

"Why not?"

"Because I knew you'd have something to say, that's why."

She was soldering together strips of thin black wire. She had done about fifteen and had them in a small pile. I asked how much she was getting paid.

"It's none of your business."

"It is."

"It bloody isn't. I've got to do something. I can't sit around here all day. It's a job, isn't it?"

I asked her a few times until she revealed she was on £1 for every fifty she soldered.

"Well, you've done fifteen, so that's 30p. How long has it taken you?"

"Nearly two hours."

"Two hours? That means you're getting paid 15p an hour."

"So. I'll get quicker as I get used to it."

I said I wouldn't work for so little and she said I was a spoiled brat and didn't have a clue what life was all about, not a clue.

When they came to collect the wire the next day, she handed back the boxes and told them not to deliver any more. And they didn't have to pay the 30p they owed her, they could keep it.

When we found the ground and parked up dad's mood changed. All that shouting and swearing already felt like an adventure; a story waiting to be told later. He now wanted to joke and skip through the streets as if he had left his irascible, bad-tempered half-brother locked in the car.

Inside the ground he settled and was wonderful company. He could read a game of football intuitively, so his comments were keen and intelligent. He taught me to notice the detail of a match. He'd see the defender rising to his feet after the ball had gone, rubbing his calf.

"He got a kick there, just as the ball was played. Their number nine did him."

If other supporters were criticising a certain player, he'd offer a different perspective.

"He's been chasing lost causes all afternoon. How can they moan when he's not had a ball to feet?"

He didn't volunteer his views to the people around him, as many supporters did. They were for me. Most fans skim-read a game of football; he read every line.

The slump in form after losing to Northwich saw Rochdale plummet down the division and play three of their last home games of the season in front of fewer than 1,000 fans at each one. They missed having to apply for re-election by two points.

Brian Green had arrived as all the previous managers did — blithe, determined, his heart on his sleeve, a belief that he could walk tall through the swamp of perpetual failure. As the months progressed, he must slowly have sensed the burden of legacy as if breathing in contaminated air.

The hot, sticky summer of 1976 was ten months ago and a lifetime away. When he accepted the job, he was sure, no doubt, that his charm and enthusiasm could extricate the club from its past: effort, heart, a game plan, a bit of luck here and there, and, suddenly, a club on fire. Now, as he drove home from Spotland each night, he will have been immersed in loneliness. The team kept losing; the ground was a mess; there was no money; the supporters were moaning; and the players let him down, match after match.

(He knew they weren't world-beaters but he expected more than this.)

Back at the office, the roof leaked; the central heating went off half way through the day for no reason; the part-time admin girl was ill again; the wooden panels in the referee's room were hanging off the wall; and the care-taker was pissed off because the bucket of sand put out for fag-ends had been knocked over in the tea room.

Rochdale's away form was resolutely abysmal. In a run of eighty consecutive league games in the late-1970s we won on just five occasions away from home. Dad and me regularly saw Rochdale lose heavily: 5–0, 4–0, 5–1, 4–1.

We'd be among a small group of visiting fans dotted around concrete-flagged terraces. We'd start by shouting encouragement when the players warmed up before the game.

"Come on, keep 'em out lads."

They didn't keep them out. They let them in. One-nil, two-nil, wasted journey. When we had possession of the ball we kicked it aimlessly. Our opponents soon realised they were playing a team bereft of confidence and skill. All they needed to do was run at us with the ball and our jittery, clumsy defenders scythed them down — penalty. The ball would be fired into our net and the momentum of taking it often carried the penalty taker in our direction. He'd raise his arm and smile sarcastically. By their third or fourth goal they became blasé about celebrating. It was only Rochdale, anyone could score against Rochdale.

Dad and me largely kept our anger to ourselves but around us supporters screamed out in disgust.

"You're a load of shit, Rochdale. I don't know why we bother."

Afterwards, chunnering and kicking at gravel on the car park, Rochdale fans passed each other shaking their heads. We were miles from home, unsure of the way back to the motorway, worried that the home supporters might attack us. And when we arrived back after a heavy defeat, people laughed and said we wanted 'locking up.'

The conditions and facilities at grounds were often dreadful too. The smell from the toilets wafted across the terraces. Most away ends were without roofs, so we got wet when it rained, often while home fans taunted us from nearby covered stands. We were served tasteless, cold pies, often from vans with serving hatches cut into their body-work. At Port Vale I saw a lad take a bite of a pie and throw-up instantly.

What made us do this? What made us hitch our fortunes to a team that left us dispirited and squalid again and again? We were an underclass of deadbeats, meeting whey-faced and forsaken on car parks in strange parts of England, lost for words, shorn of hope. What quirk of personality did we share that made us loyal to this spiteful football club?

6

Petrol Blue
Fading to Black

BRIAN GREEN HAD AN IDEA AND WAS MORE THAN happy to sit down with the man from the *Rochdale Observer* to explain all. During the previous season he had watched Manchester United reserves, a team containing six internationals, play in front of seventy people.

"How much better would it be if they played before a decent crowd in a Football League match?" he pondered. "They would be kept on their toes, they would need to be fit and they would stay sharp."

Green was arguing in favour of lower league clubs becoming 'feeder' set-ups to specific top clubs. He was making a highly speculative punt to Manchester United, suggesting Spotland was an ideal 'nursery' for their younger players and a happy home for experienced squad members short of match practice.

His 'Formula to Inspire a Soccer Revolution' came to naught although it has remained a regular hypothesis on the sporting agenda.

While many gave up on Rochdale, the boot boys stayed loyal. If we travelled to nearby grounds such as Tranmere, Crewe, Halifax, Chester, Stockport or Bury, they formed the majority of the travelling support. It meant the club had two distinct groups of fans — young men on the lookout for 'aggro' and grandads, dads, mums and kids. They stood apart on the terraces but were known to one another through family or work ties. A lad might pass, scarves around his wrists and waist, head shaved, stern expression. Someone would shout:

"Hey, Tony. How's your mum — any better?"

He'd suddenly fall sheepish, checking whether his mates were watching.

"Er, yes, she's fine now."

"Tell her I asked about her, won't you?"

"Yeah, I will."

People said the hooligans were uninterested in football and went 'just for the trouble' but their behaviour correlated to events on the field. A bombastic referee or a reckless defender chopping away at our players incurred their wrath. When we scored they were ecstatic, hugging one another madly, clenching their fists. If we conceded a goal they fell silent and watched their counterparts celebrating on the other side of the fence, hatred burning in their eyes. They might move towards them, snarling, shouting for them to shut up or they were going to get their heads kicked in.

If we were losing heavily they often left the ground to seek out rival supporters. At a match against Crewe they departed en masse about ten minutes before the end. The terraces were suddenly deserted. After a few seconds, we heard noises behind the stand—a roar, people shouting and screaming, thuds, windows smashing.

Four new players were signed in the summer of 1977. One of them was David Esser. He boasted a huge bubble perm that saw him placed to the side on the team photograph to avoid concealing players behind him.

Esser was unusually small with chunky legs. The perm almost doubled his height. We soon learned that he had an irascible temperament; in the pre-season friendlies, he ran around like a man on fire. I asked dad whether the word 'esser' meant anything. He told me it was a kind of forest creature, similar in temperament to a weasel but with sharper teeth and stronger jaws. You wouldn't want one round your legs.

Dad didn't have the same intuition as me. He was oblivious when rival supporters were among us.

"Let's move to the back," I'd say.

"Why, can't you see from here?"

"It's not that."

"What is it?"

I'd point to the gang that had assembled a few feet from where we were standing.

"They're going to start fighting in a minute."

"Aren't they Rochdale?"

"No."

At one match Cardiff City fans 'took' the Sandy Lane End. They had rushed the main body of Rochdale fans and driven them to the other side of the ground. The only Rochdale supporters remaining were older fans and kids. The Cardiff fans were disappointed that their mission had been completed so swiftly. They began picking fights on an arbitrary basis with the old-boys who remained. They would bump into one of them. The old fella, thinking it was merely an argument between him and another clumsy supporter, complained:

"Careful, lad."

Unknown to him the Cardiff fan was accompanied by others who had cunningly formed a circle and were waiting for the argument to escalate. The Cardiff fan passed his drink to a friend and put his face inches from him:

"Fucking shut it grandad."

He was bewildered and instinctively held up his arms, padding away the younger man. The Cardiff fan, satisfied that this represented defiance, punched him cleanly on the side of the face. The old man sobbed and reached in his pocket for a handkerchief to hold against his cheek.

Dad missed most of the incident but the speed of the punch caught his eye. As the fist connected and there was a dull thud, dad made a strange sound. It wasn't a word but a combination of a shout and scream. I grabbed his coat and pulled hard.

"Leave it dad."

"He's just punched that old bloke."

"I know. They're picking fights."

The Cardiff fans looked around to see who had made the

sound. They couldn't locate it and moved past us towards the centre of the stand. Dad, with a few other Rochdale supporters, tended to the old man. He was shaking and gripped the lapel of his overcoat as if stopping himself from falling apart.

Tom Mellor (Ford) Ltd became Rochdale's first ever match sponsor. Roger Fielding, the club's commercial manager, announced that they would treat a party from Mellor's to a meal at the Crimble Hotel before the League Cup tie against Halifax Town, followed by free tickets to the game.

The garage, Rochdale's main Ford dealers, promised a free Ford Fiesta valued at £2,000 to the *first* Rochdale player to score a hat-trick in the game. Since it had been seven years since anyone had last scored a hat-trick for Rochdale and fifty-one years since two Rochdale players had scored hat-tricks in the same game, there was probably no pressing need to stipulate that only the first to three goals could drive home in style.

Most of us from the street went to the youth club at St Luke's on Friday nights. We were in and out of side-rooms, bumping into one another, mock preaching from the stage or whizzing each other across the dusty floor. Fights broke out. A kid would be hurried to the toilets with a bleeding nose, a trail of red splashes behind him. Others found brushes in the stockrooms and galloped around as if they were taking part in jousting tournaments. Fluorescent tubes were waved triumphantly until a leader intervened:

"Put that away, will you? This minute. Those things can explode."

A karate club used the large room above the hall and, under no circumstances *whatsoever*, were we allowed up there. Steven Fletcher and me gave the leaders the slip one Friday. Fletcher pressed his face to the glass in the door and I sneaked a look over his shoulder. They were dressed in white baggy suits and pulled weird, strained expressions as they did their routines. Steven said they looked like they were trying to have a shit.

He started imitating them, for my benefit at first but then so they could see him. The sniggering stopped. Steven turned white. He'd been spotted by the bloke we called Karate Joe, the club leader. The door crashed open. I'd already turned to run and was flitting down the stairs when Steven passed me three feet from the ground. He hit the wall and fell in a heap. Karate Joe was at the top, shaking in rage.

"You've been told time and time again not to come up here."

"Fuck off," cried Steven, rubbing his backside.

"If you come up here again it'll be more than a boot up the arse. Do you hear me?"

"I'll get my dad on you. He won't bother with all that kung fu shit. He'll just beat you up."

At Spotland we formed acquaintances with the people sitting or standing around us. These were usually unspoken: a nod, a barely audible 'Alright?' We might overhear someone referring to them by name and, over the course of a few seasons, use it ourselves but we'd never think to ask their surnames or their jobs or anything about their family.

One season we stood close to two blokes called John who became known to me and dad as Chicken John and Bladder John. Chicken John wore a thick jacket with sheepskin — threadbare and yellowing — around the collar and across the top of two large pockets level with his thighs. At every match he'd jam pieces of chicken into these pockets, wrapped tightly in tin foil. He'd relocate to the back of the stand at half-time and disgorge the chicken from the wrapping. He moved away from the rest of us to do this as if he were taking part in a primeval ritual. When the Tannoy man fell silent, we would hear the sound of bones snapping and see John licking his lips and wiping residual fat from his hands on to his coat or the wall.

A young lad passed once who had never seen this custom before. He spoke his thoughts:

"What you doing?"

John was angered by this intrusion into what he considered a private act.

"I'm having my fucking dinner, what does it look like?"

Bladder John drank so much beer before a game that he spent most of his time shuffling across the terraces to the toilets. When he did watch the match he swayed slightly and you could sense the alcohol sloshing around his stomach as he nursed it, burping and rubbing it gently with the palms of his hands.

A minute or so before he left for the toilet, he always looked about him and shifted his weight from foot to foot.

He made everyone else feel like they wanted to go as well. He had a favourite route—across a few yards and then a left turn by the crash barrier, down to the cinder walkway at pitch level. On his third or fourth trip at one match, a fan further up the terraces shouted down:

"Hey, Shorty [Bladder John was about five ft four ins tall]. What is with you and that piss-stone?"

John didn't stop walking but moved his head drunkenly trying to trace the voice. Before he could answer, another shout came down:

"Leave the lad alone. It's probably more fun staring at a piss-stone than this lot on the pitch."

The inevitable happened. The excitable Esser over-did it. He was sent off following a punch-up just thirty minutes into the League Cup tie against Halifax Town. Referee, John Hough, revealed a novel approach to his province, telling the press afterwards:

"It was anything but a brawl. It was a well controlled free-for-all and nothing more. I shouted to the players to get involved."

The match ended a draw with Rochdale's goal coming via Alan Tarbuck's nose after the ball was struck into his face.

Geoff Morley went to the youth club even though he was nearly old enough to get into pubs. He was tall with curly red hair. He beckoned a group of us over during a break when one of the leaders pushed a trolley into the hall laden with orange juice and a huge plate of biscuits.

Morley was leaning against a radiator. He was with his mate, Carl, who never spoke but was always chuckling, at nothing.

"Come here lads, you're gonna learn something," said Morley.

We stared up.

"Do you know what a 'motty' is?"

We didn't. Geoff laughed. Carl chuckled.

"Right. Well, do you know what a 'clitoris' is?"

He said 'clitoris' slowly, hissing as he began and lengthening the word so it took him a few seconds to say. No, we didn't know what a clitoris was either.

"Thought you didn't. Well, try this. Do you know what a 'sweaty flange' is?

No.

"They're all names for a woman's fanny, dickheads."

I travelled with dad to Halifax for the second-leg of the League Cup tie. It was a late-summer's evening. We won 2–1. On the way back we passed reservoirs, forests, rough moorland. Above us, the sky was petrol blue fading to black. It felt good to win away at last.

When we arrived home the television news had just started. A piece of paper was handed to the newscaster. He paused slightly, his concentration broken.

"It is being reported that Elvis Presley, known to millions as the king of Rock 'n' Roll, has died. We will bring you more news on this as soon as we have it."

Elvis was my dad's hero, as omnipresent in our house as an older brother. His music woke us up in the morning; it drifted up the stairs at night. Dad bought the LPs when we were in Woolworth's on holiday or on day trips. He had a mirror on the landing with Elvis in his army uniform picked out in grainy dots. He shrugged.

"I've still got his records."

Soon afterwards there was another statement on the news refuting the earlier one. He might not be dead, after all. Dad set off for the pub. I was left with mum. I couldn't believe he hadn't stuck around to find out for definite.

"That's your dad for you."

We spent several seasons next to the 'wireless men', three blokes with a part-share of a tiny transistor radio. They had long expressionless faces as if they had been sculpted from a Polaroid picture while it was still wet and sticky. They watched the games but they held secondary appeal to the information gathered from the radio—probably scores from other matches. If the one with it closest to his ear (they took turns) showed a flicker of excitement, they huddled close like a doo-wop group about to start singing.

At one game we saw a cartoon come to life. When I was a kid, dad used to draw me a funny man to colour in. He did the same one all the time; it was just about the only thing he could draw. He was an old chap with a large fore-head, very few teeth, small currant eyes and a round chin. Dad did him in profile with a cigarette hanging limply out of his mouth and a trilby hat perched on the back of his head like a gangster in an old black and white film.

We were watching the match when a bloke in a long raincoat stood in front of us and looked across to the pie hut. He was wearing clothes that belonged to a different era and he fidgeted, twitching his shoulders and dipping in and out of his pockets. I looked at dad. His eyes were twinkling. We burst out laughing. It was the cartoon man.

Rochdale landed a home tie against Leeds United in the League Cup. Leeds had been League Champions three years before and European Cup finalists two years earlier. A crowd of 20,000 was expected and the game was made all-ticket. Brian Green told the press:

"It will be a sell-out, make no mistake. If it isn't then there's something wrong with football."

The *Rochdale Observer* carried a photograph of the queue at the ticket office stretching the length of the Main Stand. About thirty faces were visible on the photograph; I didn't recognise any of them.

Johno was the first in the gang to buy a CB radio. He was soon bored. He started interrupting bona fide truckers (or people living on nearby estates pretending to be bona fide truckers) while they were embroiled in jargon-strewn discussions about traffic cones and smokies [police] and the state of traffic on the motorway.

"Hey, who's there?" yelled Johno.

You were supposed to say 'ten-four for a copy' to speak to someone.

"Well good buddy, you got Bill the Bandit enjoying a good old wag with Pie Crust, just heading north of Monkey Town. Who we got on the side?"

"Me."

Condescending laughter crackled down the line.

"Yeah good buddy but who's 'me'?"

"Me, Bucket."

"Well, how do Bucket. How many candles are you burning there?"

This was code for asking your age. Before Johno could answer, Bill the Bandit spoke again:

"Could you tell me how much poundage I'm throwing you there, five-four-three-two-one." [CB'ers were continually asking the strength of their signal, it was like a verbal tic.]

"It's not my birthday," said Johno, giggling.

"No son, I'm asking how old you are."

"Why are you asking me that? Do you want to shag me or something?"

"Listen here, bucket mouth."

"Fuck off."

The laid-back Americanised singsong voice of before was replaced instantly by a blunt northern growl.

"Just get off the air will you? If I find out where you live I'm going to come round and beat the living shit out of you."

While Bill the Bandit yelled threats, Pie Crust was squealing:

"Bucket mouth on channel 17, repeat, bucket mouth on channel 17. Warning: avoid channel 17."

Johno mimicked him:

"Warning, bent bastard truckers picking up kids on channel 17. Warning, queer lorry drivers alert. Calling all cars, all cars."

I wasn't in the queue for Leeds tickets because the match fell during a week when I was going on a school holiday at an adventure centre in mid-Wales.

We hiked to the top of Cader Idris and surfed down the scree to a clear blue pool. We canoed in Mawddach estuary and played rounders in a clearing between trees on a beautiful late-summer evening. We flirted after dark with the girls, walking with them along the edge of a forest, daring ourselves to reach for their hands and make our feelings known. All the time, burning bright like the after-effect of a camera flash, I was thinking about the forth-coming game against Leeds.

It wasn't like at school; the girls were talking to us, and listening. Could we sneak a win? They were open, happy to be in our company instead of scurrying away to their friends or double Maths down the corridor. A draw maybe and a replay at Elland Road. Jackie and Kathy, and me and John went everywhere together. If we could just keep the score level for the first twenty minutes, we might grow in confidence and steal a win. I thought, for the first time, that there might be people (girls especially) who didn't mind you being quiet and a bit shy. Life might not be like it was at school, it might be okay. I arranged to phone dad on Thursday morning to find out the result.

We lost 3–0 in front of just 8,664 fans. Our usual full back, Paul Hallows, had missed the game through suspension and Ted Oliver, a 16-year-old apprentice, had taken his place. Dad said he had done his best but had been outclassed.

A group of us walked into Barmouth and I bought a newspaper. Rochdale had made back-page headlines in the *Daily Mirror*—'Oliver Twisted'.*

The two 'truckers' said they would 'take it down nine'. This meant they were moving down nine channels to resume their conversation. Johno tuned in again. It was as if they had witnessed a murder. They were whispering:

"Are you there Pie Crust?"

"I'm here."

"Are you okay?"

"Yeah, I'm fine."

"No need for it, is there?"

Johno couldn't resist. Triumphantly, he burst back into their lives.

"Hey, bummer boys, stop feeling sorry for yourselves. It's Bucket here again."

---

* The early rounds of the League Cup barely warrant a mention in the newspapers these days; it is a job to find the results listed. Top clubs treat the competition so disrespectfully that they field their fringe players until the later stages. Shame on them.

Bill the Bandit lost control.

"Fuck off will you? Just fuck off. I'm coming to get you Bucket. I know where you live."

Johno snapped the radio off; he'd heard rumours of CB'ers with 'super aerials' able to track people down.

After losing to Leeds, Brian Green conducted a press conference on the pitch at Spotland. I imagined him surrounded by reporters, the stands now empty. He shakes his head in disbelief: 8,664 fans to see Leeds United, a team packed with internationals, on a balmy August evening.

"It was disgusting," he said. "If we can't attract people to see one of the best sides in the world, what chances have we got with the bread and butter matches against Doncaster and Huddersfield? I'm very grateful to those who did come but what can we do now? I'm stuck for an answer."

When he returned to his office, leaned back in his chair and sighed, it is hard not to believe there was a knock on the door:

"Got a minute, Brian?"

Ten days later Green announced that he was leaving Rochdale to join Leeds United as manager of their reserve team. He told the players after they had lost 3–0 at Swansea City, a defeat that left them at the bottom of the Football League. He said the club had 'a basis of a side that could do well in the Fourth Division once it had been moulded together.'

Thinking of home and Dale, Barmouth, 1977.

7

The Joy of Small Things

WHEN MUM AND DAD FILLED IN THE FORMS FOR THE holiday, they probably hadn't noticed particularly that it was held at a Christian centre.

After a few days there we made friends with two men in their early twenties, Andy and Clive, who were also on holiday. They played games with us and it didn't feel odd that they were about ten years older than us. They were gentle and trusting and cheerful. They told us they were Christians and a group of us started going round to their chalet, asking them about God and the Bible.

On the last night Andy read us a poem called *Footprints*, about a man who dreamt he was walking along a beach with God while scenes from his life flashed across the sky. During the saddest times the man noticed there was only one set of footprints.

"He asked whether God had forsaken him," said Andy. "God replied that he would never leave him and during times of trial and suffering, when he could see only one set of footprints, it was because he had carried him."

He closed the book and as its covers came together we heard snuffling. Stephen Killroy was crying. Andy and Clive went to comfort him and we scrambled to the edge of the bed to watch.

"Is he okay?"

"He'll be all right in a minute," said Clive.

"What's upset you Killy?" asked Jackie.

"It's what Andy's just read out, that story."

He was looking around the room as if surprised to find himself there. Darkness was fanning in through the doors and windows, the sun now blood red and tired over the estuary. Something strange and brilliant had happened and we all sensed it.

"That story, it's beautiful isn't it?"

I'd never heard a kid say the word 'beautiful' before. He started sobbing again and Clive held him. None of us giggled or mocked him, not even when we were back at school again and it had all felt like a dream.

At the beginning of the 1977–78 season I started a scrapbook dedicated to Rochdale AFC. I glued a team photograph on the cover and a picture of Brian Green. Colour photographs weren't available so I coloured them by hand, neatly applying felt tip to their kits, the grass, Green's polo neck jumper and the players' hair. Using letters cut from different newspapers—much like a kidnap demand—I formed 'Rochdale Rule OK' and wrote in black ink: 'Rochdale The Mighty Blues.'

The cuttings were comprehensive until mid-September

but then stopped, with the last few pages left blank. The final articles revealed the source of my sudden disaffection: 'County go for striker', 'Reading and Mountford in transfer talks' and 'Huddersfield Sign Mountford—Reading pipped at post.'

On Thursday September 29, 1977, Bob Mountford left Rochdale to join Huddersfield Town for a £10,000 transfer fee. In almost three seasons he had scored thirty-seven goals in ninety-seven full appearances for Rochdale, a remarkable goals-per-game ratio considering the mediocre side he had played in.

While those around him were routinely listless and useless, Mountford had volunteered a foot, a thigh, a forehead or a dig in the ribs. When he scored he did not look surprised or scamp around like a bolted foal but held up his arm regally like a man who knew he was born to play football and score goals. He didn't run to the supporters or court their affections; they could see for themselves that he wore the shirt with pride.

Other players had moved on but my emotional investment in them had been meagre by comparison. Bob Mountford *was* Rochdale, one of only a few who looked as if they really belonged on a football field.

Dad and me and Rochdale and Bob Mountford were supposed to be forever. How could he wear another club's shirt? How could he raise aloft an arm to salute a goal for anyone but Rochdale? The kit fitted him so well, the stripes down the sleeve, the blue and the white. And what was Janet Marcroft to do with her home-made badge? Bob Mountford might eat *our* goalie now.

Back home, I joined a Christian youth group that met in the basement of a church in town. I turned up one Friday evening and sat among these kids and grown-ups I'd never met before. Candles were on the tables and the flickering light lit up pastel drawings on the wall depicting Bible stories. I told them my name and they asked me to pull up a chair and join the discussion. I wasn't shy or self-aware; going into there felt the same as walking from one room to another at home.

In the space of a few weeks I'd come to understand. It did feel as if I was *born-again* and that Jesus Christ had *entered my life,* phrases I'd heard Andy and Clive say on the holiday. I had an extraordinary sense of wellbeing made up of conflicting elements: energy and serenity, confidence and humility, and it came without side effects or at a price. If you *believed* you were granted this self-assurance and happiness, the joy of small things, a love for others. You were all the things you ever wanted to be, all the time.

We couldn't leave it there, couldn't let go. Huddersfield was only about twenty miles away. On Boxing Day, 1977, we travelled to see them play against Southend United.

When Mountford had played for Rochdale we watched him closely but ultimately viewed him as part of the team. At Huddersfield he was more or less the whole game for us. We felt a sense of responsibility as if he was still representing Rochdale though he wore different colours. We wanted him to play well so fans would nudge one another, enthuse, and it reflect favourably on Rochdale.

Mum and dad didn't understand.

"How do you mean, *born-again*?"

I explained that it wasn't a physical birth but an entry into another life. Mum was sceptical.

"I thought we were all Christians anyway. Me and your dad got you christened when you were a baby. Wasn't that enough?"

I said she shouldn't take it personally.

"Hey, don't get too full of yourself."

I said I'd pray to Jesus Christ, our saviour, and ask him to spare her soul. She saw I was joking and got up from the settee.

"Pack it in."

Later she asked now I was into all this religion and everything, did it mean I was going to do more jobs around the house? I could start by peeling the potatoes. I said it didn't work like that.

"Aha," she shouted victoriously. "Got you."

I asked what she meant. She nodded, smiling.

"You're into this religion to suit yourself, aren't you?"

She waved her finger and laughed.

Dad never really spoke about it. He listened and said it was up to me; it was my life. Mum released snippets of information on his behalf:

"He's not sure it's the kind of thing that lads your age are supposed to be involved with."

The game no longer made sense without the periphery; it was like tunnel vision. We were nervous for Mountford, as if we were playing too. A fierce eye trained on one player seemed to force mistakes upon him. Mountford, of course, was a natural, playing football was his trade. He settled after a few minutes and played as well as he had done for Rochdale. Our worries were unfounded.

Shortly before the end there was a scramble in the penalty area and, as always, he was first to the ball, driving it beyond the Southend goalkeeper. The roar was louder than at Spotland and fans cascaded down the terracing behind the goal. We were swept along but before I was forced to look down and check my steps, I made a final glance at the pitch. Mountford had his arms outstretched victoriously. The goal had made it 2–0 and sealed the win. Mud was spattered across his face and shirt. His new team-mates clung to his arms and back. The floodlights were on. Mountford glowed beneath them like a struck match.

Ralph was the most popular leader at St Luke's. He wore jeans and check shirts and rode a motorbike. He'd talk us through the bike's machinery, pointing to the spark plugs and carburettor, explaining how it all worked. A large leather crucifix dangled from his neck.

As we were leaving one Friday night he asked if I'd like to go to his house the next day and help him wallpaper the front room.

"It would be a lot easier with two."

I took two buses to reach his bungalow. His motorbike was parked in front of the garage. He opened the door, smiling broadly. A few buttons on his shirt were undone and he had a white T-shirt underneath.

The house was extremely tidy. A large tapestry of a dove flying past a cross was on the wall above the gas fire. Beneath the picture it said: 'Jesus is Life.'

"I'll put the kettle on," he said.

I told him I'd prefer lemonade or orange, if he had any.

"I think I have, I think I have," he said as if he was singing along to notes on a piano.

We worked well together. I cut the paper to length, pasted it, and he put it on the wall. He had small, supple fingers and stuck out his tongue as he brought the edges together.

He told me about himself. He'd been a biker and used to drink heavily with his mates. He kept saying, 'I liked a drink,' and staring at me earnestly. He told me he used to 'travel all over' and 'meet all kinds of people.' He was wearing tartan carpet slippers.

"Do you know what changed? Do you know who made me see where I had gone wrong?" he asked.

I shook my head.

"The Lord. He spoke to me. He tapped me on the shoulder and he said 'What are you doing with your life? Where are you going?'"

He glared at me:

"Do you know why I've asked you here today?"

He still had the pasting brush in his hand and was waving it as he spoke. The bucket of paste was behind him and I thought if he took another step back he might stand in it. He asked me again:

"Do you want to know why?"

I shrugged.

"I asked you here because I have the feeling you want to talk about Christ. I mean — really talk. Am I right?"

He was making me uncomfortable. When I didn't answer immediately, a look of disappointment fell across his face as if he'd suffered a stroke.

"Well, that's up to you but I'm here when you do. And I'll always be here."

He said this as if he was rallying himself. We didn't speak for a while and I had the impression I'd upset him.

Rochdale lost ten of their first twelve games of the season. Letters appeared in the *Rochdale Observer* criticising the Board's reluctance to speculate and for selling the best players. A letter-writer calling himself JBS wrote (rather clumsily): 'They [Rochdale supporters] know nothing because they don't know anything, only failure. Who in their right mind would put money into the club knowing the return would be 'no return'?'

A blind girl called Joanne often attended the meetings with her guide dog. When we sat around discussing Jesus Christ, our Saviour, she tilted back her head as if looking for light, smiling as she listened. One night the conversation turned to what television programmes we liked and she said her favourite was *Starsky and Hutch*.

"I like it too," said one of the others.

"Why do you like it Joanne?" asked the lay-preacher.

She blushed and bent down as if to stroke her dog.

"Come on, tell us," he teased.

"I fancy David Soul," she blurted.

"Do you?"

One of the kids looked bemused:

"How can you fancy him Joanne, when you can't see him?"

"It's his voice. I can just tell he's kind and nice."

Mike Ferguson, Rochdale's former captain, was appointed caretaker-manager in September 1977. He was the converse of Green: sallow complexion, hunched shoulders, the collar of his washed-out tracksuit turned up to meet huge sideburns. He looked like a school caretaker, head bowed, muttering that the fifth-form boys hadn't put away the mats in the gym.

He was thirty-four but would have passed for older beneath the stands in the gloom of a late November afternoon. He had played at a higher level and was known for an enterprise and vision that mocked his demeanour. He announced that he wanted to imbue Rochdale with some of his old playing style:

"If a player wants to flip the ball up and juggle it on to his shoulder —great, that's what I like to see, because the player has got confidence."

I was happy going to the meetings, the youth groups and the get-togethers at houses but they kept pressing the point, confounded that I still hadn't found myself a church.

At one meeting I was sitting cross-legged on the floor (we'd formed a circle), feeling pretty good about myself because I'd caught the bus in the pouring rain and found this house on an estate miles from anywhere. A bloke in a denim shirt and a trimmed beard was sitting on the settee. He came right out and asked. I didn't know he knew who I was. He called me by my name and asked if I'd started to attend church *yet*.

"Nope," I said breezily, hoping he'd sense I didn't want to talk about it.

"You should do really."

I smiled and said I felt okay.

"I'm not sure you can consider yourself a Christian if you don't go to church."

I suddenly felt homesick. He softened and did this forced twitchy smile that made his beard go up and down.

"Honestly, it's fantastic in church. It's where we all feel as one with God. It's like, instead of visiting your friends' houses which is cool and everything, you're visiting God's house. It's where his love exists, where you can feel it strongest."

At the point when he'd said 'cool and everything' I looked around to see if anyone else had noticed how disingenuous it sounded on his lips. No one glanced back. I was also wondering why Christian blokes wore either check or denim shirts, as if it was a uniform.

Craig Jenkins was one of only a handful from school who also supported Rochdale. He was a normal, quiet kid until he got to a football match. He stood in the Willbutts Lane stand and we'd often see him break free from the main body of supporters, race down, and hurl abuse at a linesman or the referee. My dad tapped me on the arm at one match:

"I think Craig's lost it."

He was always losing it. Usually, one of the people he stood among coaxed him back, away from harm's way. If I ventured over to that side of the ground, perhaps for a pie or to use the toilet, I'd see the scene played out. Craig would look as if he was going to climb over the wall and make his point directly to the referee. In his excitable state he hardly made sense:

"You, yer bastard. That, then, it were never offside. Here, have my glasses."

He'd pull off his glasses and wave them extravagantly. They were old fashioned with thick black frames. When he took them off he blinked and squinted. A mate pulled at his arm:

"Craig, leave it."

"Leave it, leave it? This bastard's biased. He hates Rochdale. We've not had a decision all day."

"Craig, you're going to get in trouble."

"I don't care. I want a word with the ref now."

One or two police officers ambled over.

"Come on, son. Just get back to where you were will you and leave it."

"It's that ref, he hates Rochdale."

"He might do but we can't have you threatening him, can we?"

"He wants threatening."

On one occasion Craig was actually arrested. He was hauled over the fence by a copper and frog-marched around the pitch with his arm pushed up his back. I was close to the fence but didn't expect him to notice me. He came to within a few yards:

"Hiya, how you doing?" he said.

"All right."

Instinctively, I added:

"You're not doing too good."

"I deserve it. I lost it completely back there. He's only doing his job."

Craig was soon a few yards away. He shouted back:

"Do you think we'll win?"

I didn't know whether to run alongside the fence continuing the conversation or shout back. Luckily he saw someone else he knew in the crowd and began talking to him instead.

During his last few days at Rochdale, Brian Green had signed a striker he had been chasing through the summer. Terry Owen was unhappy at Cambridge United and wanted to join a club closer to his home town of Chester.

On his debut against Brentford the *Rochdale Observer* reported that he showed, 'selfless running and sweet ball play'. He scored Rochdale's only goal in a 2–1 home defeat, out-jumping the much taller visiting defender, Pat Kruse.

As we were to discover years later, Owen's play was similar in style to his son, Michael.*

Finally, I went to the church nearest our house. A few pensioners were sitting in the front pews while the vicar got himself ready at the side, flattening down his hair and thumbing through papers he'd inserted into a Bible.

The building was cold because the sun hadn't risen high enough to send light through the tall windows. Before he started the vicar looked towards the back as if double-checking that no one else would be joining us. I sat half way down and had a pew to myself. One or two old ladies turned round and smiled.

His voice reverberated through the room and I could barely hear what he was saying. He spoke in a monotone and kept his body perfectly still. When he looked up from his notes it was perfunctory as if he'd been told it was a good technique. The hymn numbers were set in a wooden frame at the side of the pulpit. When the singing began it was a cheerless drone without any recognisable tune.

Afterwards, as the pensioners filed out, they each looked over, grinning and nodding. The vicar was fast on his feet, his cassock flowing as he zipped down the aisle to greet me.

"Hello," he said. "I don't think I've seen you here before."

---

* Rochdale has a reputation for fielding players with famous progeny. The fathers of two of England's 1966 World Cup winning team played for the club, albeit briefly: Charlie Hurst (father of Geoff) in 1946 and Alan Ball Snr in 1951. On a similar theme, John Stiles (son of Nobby) spent a month on loan to the club in March 1991.

"No, it's my first time."

"Are you new to the area?"

I noticed some of the ladies had stopped and were craning their necks to hear. I was embarrassed by the attention.

"No, I've lived around here for a bit."

He wanted to ask more but I'd already partially turned away. As I shuffled between the pews, he raised his hand to wave:

"I hope we'll see you again soon."

That afternoon I caught a bus to a youth group on the other side of town. I told them about the church. They said I should go with them to their church which had a 'modern outlook'. They played guitars and sang and the vicar was a real character. I didn't like the sound of that either.

Rochdale lost six out of seven games while Ferguson was 'acting manager' but he was still given the job. The formal announcement was made before an away match at Northampton Town.

I imagined his pre-match team-talk. It was a fresh start. They were *his* players now and in the team because he felt they were good enough and honest enough to do a job. Northampton were having an indifferent season, so he will have told them to keep it tight, hold their shape and take the sting out of their play in the first fifteen minutes. After that, they were to push forward and see if they could steal something from the game. Come on lads, go out there and show 'em.

Rochdale conceded a goal after thirty-three seconds. They lost 3–1.

8

When Dreams
Became Flesh

WITHIN A YEAR AND LIKE SUNBURN FADING OVER winter months, I lost my faith. I stopped going to the church groups and reading my *New Testament* at the end of each day.

I wanted to leave behind the people I'd met as a Christian. Their blithe, open lives and bright-lit eyes now made me uneasy. Their happiness depressed me. There felt to be a conceit about them as if they already knew the punch line but let you tell the joke all the same, acting as if it was the first time they'd heard it.

No longer did I want to sit in dusty halls on plastic chairs while day turned to night outside. I was tired of the sound of tambourines and chinking coffee cups and the rigmarole of communal washing up and checking diaries to organise the next meeting.

Mum and dad probably noticed but didn't mention it. Maybe they thought it might prompt me to turn back to my old ways. They still teased me with 'go and look in your bloody Bible' if I asked them an awkward question or 'you're supposed to be religious,' whenever I did something they considered nefarious, such as leaving my bedroom untidied. They probably viewed it as a schoolboy fad like skateboarding or collecting Top Trumps.

A few of us cycled to Spotland although it wasn't a match night. It was in darkness except for a small lamp issuing a dreary splash of light over the main entrance. Posters advertising long gone matches were glued to the brickwork. They had been partially washed down, their top corners curled over.

The rain had fallen all day and deep puddles formed in ruts on the car park. A rusty brazier was yards from the turnstile where we usually entered the ground. I felt the sides; it was still warm. Old programmes were jammed inside. I poked at this dense pile and they turned to dust, swirling in the wind like moths back from the dead.

I found another pile on the floor. Their edges were black and serrated as if they had been dipped into the flames and withdrawn again. They were now wet and soggy. I thumbed through hoping to find some that weren't damaged. Dave Taylor, my mate, saw me:

"What you doing?"

"Seeing if any are still okay."

He climbed off his bike and tilted it to the floor on its side.

"Here, let's have a look."

He took another handful and began peeling them apart. Tiny slugs were trapped between some of them.

"I think you're out of luck."

"I know."

He knew what I was thinking.

"It's a shame, isn't it?"

Once more Rochdale were drawn against a non-League club in the first round of the FA Cup. Scarborough were top of the Northern Premier League and considered favourites. Ferguson responded frostily:

"They may fancy their chances but it's Rochdale who are going through to the next round, possibly by three or four goals."

Rochdale lost 4–2. 'Shameful Dale' was the headline in the *Rochdale Observer*. Its match report said the club was a 'sad ambassador for League football.' Ferguson summed up the performance as 'diabolical.'

The team against Scarborough had included Steven Shaw who had just turned 17-years-old. Ted Oliver did not play in the cup-tie but was regularly called upon in the league despite being sixteen. These were not prodigious talents too gifted to restrict to youth and reserve team football. They were raw youngsters, willing to run and chase but ultimately making up the numbers. They were also exceptionally frail, particularly Oliver, who was under ten stone. Theirs was a hopeless assignment: playing alongside dispirited senior players who were perpetually under attack, on pitches thick with mud, against men of much

There is a light that never goes out.

greater physical strength. In most games they weren't beaten, they were flattened.

My dad set up a junior football club made up of kids either living nearby or going to my school. His own dad had run one before him, so I think he considered it a sort of family business. He was an unlikely person to run a team, far too shy really. At first I was ambivalent about the idea. It meant I could play regularly but being the manager's son set me apart from the other lads. Before long I began to resent the situation. I wanted my parents to be like everyone else's — hidden. And dad couldn't get the basic stuff right, like making them be quiet and listen while he was talking. They were never overtly cheeky or arrogant but I watched their faces and listened for every comment. I was terrified of them being sarcastic, not sure whether I should join in or stay quiet.

We didn't train properly. He'd throw us the ball and tell us to 'enjoy ourselves'. There were no team talks, just awkward gee-ups where dad and his pal, Harry Whitworth, said, 'You can beat these', or 'Come on lads, give it your best.'

The matches were on Sunday mornings and the players met outside our house. They were supposed to turn up for 9 am but some arrived half an hour early. I'd come downstairs in my pyjamas and see their outline through the frosted glass in the front door as they slumped on the doorstep. I never opened the door or acknowledged them. I didn't want them there. I hated that I was separated from them, made to feel special and delicate. When we left and drove to play the match, it took about an hour before I felt I was one of the gang.

On a job, dad met someone who knew Rochdale's captain, Nigel O'Loughlin. Dad contacted him and he agreed to become our coach, forming half of a new management team alongside a teacher from school, Mr Smithies. They were a bizarre alliance.

Mr Smithies was tall, thin, bald and bespectacled with a gentle manner and a soft lisp. The lenses of his glasses were thick and had a slight purple tint. He had a way of lifting his eyebrows and making a coy expression that suggested he thought his eyes twinkled more than they actually did. He tried not to — and everyone could tell he was trying — but spoke condescendingly to people like my dad and Harry Whitworth.

O'Loughlin was a stocky man with fair hair and flat, milky-blue eyes. He was a journeyman footballer with a capacity for hard work. We soon found out that he was awkward to be with, as if he was mad about something but you weren't sure what. He had an expression that was a sulk see-sawing with a sneer. On the occasions he laughed, however, it disarmed his face; you wanted to laugh with him.

Before he became a teacher Smithies had supposedly suffered an industrial accident that left him with extremely small feet. He wore special shoes and walked with short steps that caused him to sashay as he made his way down the corridors. Two versions of how he received his injury circulated the school: that a piece of sheet metal sliced off his toes and his hair fell out. Or, alternatively, that a piece of metal had fallen on his head and his toes dropped off.

In the circumstances it might have been wise for Smithies to sit out the five-a-side matches at the end of the training sessions. Instead he pulled on his extremely tight Sheffield Wednesday kit [he was a fan] and away he went, tip-toeing into tackles with a dainty precision, sidling crab-like across the pitch, sweating extravagantly. Within seconds, his face was on fire, smoke rising in thick flumes from his head. O'Loughlin joked that one of us should run a few yards behind with a brush mopping up the sweat.

Really, we should have admired his pluckiness. He was overcoming a disability, giving his best. O'Loughlin watched, his mouth partially open, eyes narrow. He was moving his head slowly from side to side as he viewed Smithies' calamitous endeavours. The taciturn one was saying, without moving his lips: 'Prick.'

I wrote a letter to Bob Mountford*. He took a month to reply. In the meantime he had moved from Huddersfield Town and was now playing at Halifax Town. I was surprised by the neatness of the writing. He wrote that it was

---

* I nicked this idea of writing to footballers and football clubs from my mate, Stephen Hewitt. His ambitions spanned the globe. He had signed photos and souvenirs from clubs such as Honved and Borussia Mönchengladbach, and had regular communication with England's goalkeeper, Peter Shilton. I built up correspondence with the characters who populated my world; hob-nail tin bath footballers — Fred Binney, Tommy Tynan, Alan Young, and, of course, Alex McGregor (see later reference).

Nigel O'Loughlin, the taciturn one.

'very nice' to receive my letter and to see I had taken such an interest in his career. He said he had made a lot of friends at Rochdale. When he had the chance to move to Huddersfield he did not hesitate because, as I knew, Huddersfield were quite a fashionable club and seemed geared for higher football. However, after a couple of months he found he was not really settled, realising that the more fashionable clubs were not always the friendliest. He finished by providing information for my *Bob Mountford File*: Bob Latchford was his favourite player; the Victoria Ground, Stoke, was his best ground; and he had been sent off four times in his career.

His next letter was in different handwriting and included his home address. The letters were tall and wavy, the lines sloping. His girlfriend or wife had probably done the first note. I imagined him taking my letter out of his kit bag one evening and showing it to her. They probably didn't write letters often, so it was a chore to find the paper and pen, and time to respond. I could see him pacing the floor of their recently-built house (it was a drive, which made it sound more modern than a street or avenue), dictating to her in the starched manner of someone not used to writing. I was proud that he had trusted me with his home address. He was more candid than before. He thought the downfall of Rochdale was the appointment of Brian Green and that Walter Joyce was a better manager.

Mountford's final letter came in an envelope lined with crinkly pink paper. It was three sides long and mainly given over to additional information for the *Bob Mountford File*. I'm not sure how grand he expected this to be but it was basically a piece of A4 paper on to which I'd typed lots of information, with his photograph and autograph on the reverse. I learned that he drove a Ford Escort; enjoyed roast duck and orange sauce; his favourite singers were Elton John and Gladys Knight; and his favourite actor was Donald Sutherland. Ominously, he closed his letter: 'I might see you at Rochdale at one of the night games. Don't be afraid of introducing yourself if you see me, then we can have a chat.'

Mike Ferguson, much the same as Brian Green had done before him, began to lament on the size of the squad. He had good reason. The official team photograph for the 1977/78 season had on it: eight full-time professionals; three apprentices (Shaw, Oliver and Ian Bannon); and two amateurs (Billy Boslem and Chris Shyne, effectively trialists).

The problem was compounded when Dave Esser, Paul Hallows and Bob Scott were sent off early in the season, causing acute manpower shortages when the suspensions came into force. Scott actually received two bans, one for being sent off and the other for shouting abuse to the referee as he left the field.

I compiled a neatly typed 10-page programme for each of our home matches in the Spotland and District Junior League, working to my own strict deadlines. In the first I included a history of the club (all three months of it), details of every player and match reports of our friendly games. I kept meticulous statistics, even the goal-per-game ratios of each player. No news item was considered too small to mention: 'Ian McMahon has changed his boots to Stylo Matchmakers this season.' I designed a club crest and drew it on the front of each programme, shading it with coloured pencils. The sheen of professionalism was dented by the occasional quirk: 'Due to a misunderstanding by both managers, we had to use rugby posts instead of football posts in the match against Deans Pursuit.' In another programme I announced that Keith Johnson had left the club because, 'he wanted to go motorbike scrambling on Sunday mornings with his mum's new boyfriend.' I didn't show the programmes to anyone, apart from Paul Foster, one of my best mates from school and the team's 'utility man'. He did the colouring-in when I was behind schedule.

I was sitting in the Main Stand with my dad before a match. Mountford, in tight nylon trousers and a woolly tartan jacket, climbed the stairs looking for somewhere to sit. He was probably on one of his routine suspensions and had decided to visit his old club. He was with a man of a similar age. The stand, as usual, was almost empty. He had the choice of hundreds of seats. He sat next to me. My dad asked if I was going to tell him who I was.

"No," I said and begged him to keep quiet.

"But you've been writing to him."

"No."

"He won't mind having a chat."

"Please dad, don't say anything."

I couldn't bring myself to look in Mountford's direction.

When we attacked the goal to my left, which was where he was sitting, I watched without moving my head so that our eyes had no possibility of meeting. I was too nervous of saying something I'd regret. While I could be passably funny and engaging in a letter, in person I was a quiet, tense teenager. I didn't want Mountford — a brave, skilful footballer *and* with the decency to write to strangers — to see the real me.

Rochdale AFC revealed in 1978 that the weekly wage bill was £1,500. It clearly wasn't enough and an exodus began. Dick Mulvaney* had already returned to his previous job in a shipyard where he said he could earn more. Steve Melledew signed for Hillingdon Borough, many rungs down the non-League ladder but apparently paying higher salaries.

"I'll be heartbroken to leave the club but I can't afford to play for Rochdale on what I'm on," he said.

Alan Vest returned to Australia and was soon joined by trainer, Frank Campbell. Mike Poole, the goalkeeper, left to join Portland Timbers in the United States, with whom he had spent the previous summer. Bobby Hoy, a tricky winger, announced that he was leaving to concentrate on a singing career.

"My heart's not in football anymore," he said.

He revealed that he was from a musical family; his sister

---

* Poor Dick, having a name like that. It sounds like something you go to the doctor with, unless your doctor is female and then you dip it in warm water for a few weeks and hope it gets better on its own.

had sung the theme tune to the television programme, *The Sky's The Limit*.

Poole's place in goal was taken by 18-year-old Andy Slack who had been working as a sorter in a tannery in Heywood. He shared the position with Chris Shyne, a stalwart of the Rochdale pub leagues whose registration was secured from his former club, the Dyers Arms.

During the 1970s football coaching was dominated by work rate with ball skills almost a peripheral matter. Nigel O'Loughlin was of his era. We began his training sessions by running across the pitch. He varied the routine half way through: we ran *around* the pitch. His closing workout was a sprint to the edge of the penalty area, jog back, sprint to the half-way line, jog back, then sprint to the goal-line at the other end.

At least we saw a ball briefly when we played in the sports hall. O'Loughlin was a devotee of two-touch football, proceeding to one-touch. He probably also considered no-touch, whereby the ball was abandoned completely but we moved around beautifully.

I soon realised that my reveries — all the romantic guff about lengthening shadows beneath the gasometer — meant nothing when dreams became flesh. There was nothing romantic or poetic about O'Loughlin or, I surmised, the rest of the Rochdale players. It was about graft; getting your foot in, closing the space, playing the simple ball. It became purely a physical activity, running until you felt ill, running until you were bored. He told us once about a player who had been sick on the training pitch through sheer effort and he saw this as a badge of honour. Some of the team thrived under him, the lads who followed his mantra of perpetual toil. In return they received the odd wink or ruffle of the hair. They glowed afterwards.

Before his arrival I had formed an agreeable niche. I was a goal-hanger. I had developed the knack of scoring, chiefly because I loitered so close to the opponents' goal area. The rest of the team scrapped for the ball, passed it to me and I usually scored. I was the one patted on the back by jubilant team-mates as we left the pitch, followed by post-match tributes from Jack Sprowell, a council gardener, a football savant and the father of our full back, Carl:

"He's just like Jimmy Greaves, isn't he?"

Life was sweet.

Rochdale's dire form meant they were condemned to a re-election application with nine games of the 1977/78 season still remaining. They had been bottom of the Football League since mid-September and didn't win away from home all season, drawing just two and losing the other twenty-one games.

It was an inauspicious way to mark their 50th season as a member of the Football League but at least they had shown dependability—they had finished bottom in their first season.

At first O'Loughlin suggested I could 'contribute' more. He wanted me to drop back a little, make some space for myself. I knew the code: he wanted me to chase about like the rest, perhaps even win the ball for myself. A week later Mr Smithies patted down the pile of his corduroy trousers and stared at me earnestly from his purple-tinged world:

"Now, I can imagine some disquiet about this but I feel that you have all the makings of a midfield player."

I loved football but I didn't love *this*. They were hacking at me from all sides. I had two seconds on the ball before a pub player passing himself off as thirteen slammed his boots into my shins. When I'd been a striker I could drift towards the wing and find dry land but the mud in the middle was past my ankles, the squelch probably audible from the other side of the park. We were the smallest team in the league, playing against lads with thighs—we had shins that went all the way up. I'd hit the floor with just enough time to see the referee waving play on as I swallowed another mouthful of soil.

Mr Smithies had an idiosyncratic way of imparting information. You were not quite up to pace, struggling to get your foot in, or the pitch didn't bring out the best in you. He might ask if you were feeling unwell, you didn't seem yourself today. I was incredulous the first time I was substituted. I looked behind as he pointed; surely he was singling out another player. One of the other lads had to confirm it.

"I think he means you."

The pain was immediate and intense. I was expected to jog to the touchline and shake hands with my replacement but my bottom lip was quivering and I had a tight ache across the top of my chest. The other side of the white line was a very still, cold place after all the running, chasing and kicking. For the first time I noticed the dried mud on my knees. My boots felt heavy and cumbersome at my feet. I was thrown a tracksuit top but my fingers were stiff and felt like someone else's as I struggled with the zip. I was unable to move towards my dad. He was pretending to watch the match, afraid of glancing in my direction. He will have been hurting too. This was supposed to be fun, a few lads from school getting together at the weekend, having a kick-about, having a laugh.

Simon Thompson, my replacement, wasn't much of a player. Out there today, he was magnificent. He was scrapping, fighting, tackling, clenching his fists. The collection of mums and dads along the touchline were singing rhapsodies to his talent. A few yards away, a 13-year-old boy who had scored *eight* goals against Spotland Rovers earlier in the season felt like a wisp of smoke about to be blown away.

The last few games of the 1977/78 season drew paltry crowds; at eight of them the figure was below 1,000. The lowest was 734 against Reading, although it also failed to exceed 800 against Torquay United and Grimsby Town.

Wisely, the club falsified these figures, usually settling on a number between 1,000 and 1,050. Although this meant the club paid more tax, it saved them revealing the depth in the fall-off of support. Regular attendances below 1,000 would have attracted adverse publicity and hindered the re-election bid.

Dad was in turmoil. He was responsible for bringing O'Loughlin and Smithies to the club and had unwittingly brought about the demotion of his son from star striker to helping Eunice Copestick chop up the half-time oranges.

In football parlance O'Loughlin and Smithies hadn't 'fancied me' and had wrested me from the team in stages. It was a routine strategy (although I'm sure it wasn't malicious): a player is singled out and certain elements of his play questioned. He is asked to play in a different position, knowing his confidence will be undermined and his natural game compromised. He might, for example, be right-footed and be asked to play on the left. In most cases, he struggles. The manager can then stand back, arms folded, head shaking and announce ruefully:

"Look, he's still struggling and after all I've done to accommodate him in the team."

Paul Foster wanted to be an engineer but when I chose to do typing lessons, believing it would help my chances of becoming a writer, he asked if he could drop metalwork so we could be together. We sat at the back and were fussed over by the teacher, Miss Savage. She'd never taught boys before and was constantly chiding herself when she forgot us:

"Right girls, let's get going." She'd flick out her right

arm to admonish herself, pawing the air: "Sorry, you gentlemen at the back. Just a slip of the tongue."

The girls turned to look. Paul pulled a funny face and slid his National Health glasses to the end of his nose:

"You naughty, naughty teacher."

Paul had a younger sister and a brother, Mark, who was about ten. He was a sweet kid, mischievous and fidgety. When I first met him it was obvious he was ill. His skin was yellow-green and he spoke in a deep voice that sometimes broke up. He had a form of leukaemia where the chances of getting better were remote. Paul told me this but I'd look at Mark charging through the house, bobbing up to the front room window to see if anyone was coming, and I couldn't believe it: how could this much energy ever be extinguished?

The two brothers slept in the same room, Mark with his bed against the window and Paul on the other side in an old wooden double bed. If we were playing a game, Mark was usually at our shoulder eager to join in.

"Can I play? I won't mess it up, honest."

Quite often his voice became a dry croak because of the drugs he was taking and if you didn't know him, it might have sounded scary coming from a little kid. Paul told him he couldn't play, we were in the middle of something.

"Go on," he pleaded.

"No, bugger off will you and find a mate your own age."

"Right, I'm going to tell my mum."

He'd walk on to the landing and wait for a few seconds. We could hear that he hadn't gone downstairs. He'd come back in.

"I've had a word with mum and she says you've got to let me play or you've had it."

"We know you're lying," said Paul.

"I'm not, that's what she said. She did. Honest."

Paul pretended to chase Mark and he jumped on his bed to escape.

"When mum gets back from the shops I'm going to tell her about you," yelled Mark.

"So she's at the shops is she? How could you have just spoken to her then?"

"Get lost will you? Just get lost," said Mark, burying his face in the bedclothes.

Mark started to spend a lot of time in hospital. He was having blood transfusions and they were hoping to find a bone marrow donor. His parents had stickers in their car windows about appeals the hospital was running.

After training one evening we gathered around O'Loughlin's car. He wound down the window and told us where to meet for the next match. Just as he prepared to drive off, I succumbed. The song was being played constantly on the radio at the time. Eventually someone foolhardy and reckless was going to sing XTC's *Making Plans for Nigel* to our resident professional footballer, someone desperate to prove that he wasn't wet or snooty because his dad ran the team they all played for. We were, after all, making plans with Nigel. He looked at me, eyes dead in their sockets:

"Not funny, just not funny," he said and accelerated out of the car park.

He was only joking.

We had been out on the Sunday that Mark died. Paul had called a few times but it was early evening and had gone dark when he caught us in. He didn't cry when he told us but his eyes were red and the skin around them swollen. My dad said, 'Sorry, son', and mum went into the kitchen to make a cup of tea; she didn't want us to see her crying.

After playing *Striker* and *Subbuteo* for a couple of hours it was time for him to go. We lingered at the front door. I didn't want him to leave and asked him to stay the night. I more or less pushed him back into the house and made my mum and dad say in front of him that he could stop over.

"Of course you can stay. You're always welcome here."

He thanked my dad using his first name (I'd never heard any of my friends do this before) but said he'd better get home. Back on the doorstep, Paul said he had to get used to Mark not being there, that it was important to get on with life again; his dad had been talking to him. He left and I watched him disappear up the road. Mum had told him to walk down the main road where it was well lit, but I knew he'd go down the canal bank.

9

Not the Centre or
Soul of the Party

WIGAN ATHLETIC WERE ELECTED TO THE FOOTBALL
League in the summer of 1978. On hearing the news, many
assumed it would be Rochdale they replaced.

Although we had finished seven points behind
Southport, they were voted out instead. Their 'previous
convictions' had obviously been taken into consideration.
They had finished second-from-bottom for three consecutive seasons. They too had suffered staff shortages and in
one game had been forced to play an outfield player in goal.

Southport were the fourth side in nine years to lose their
League place, following on from Bradford Park Avenue,
Barrow and Workington. The lobby to make the passage
between the Football League and non-League more fluid
was clearly holding sway and another disastrous season for
Rochdale would almost certainly see them jettisoned from
the League.

Rap (Rochdale's Alternative Press) was often on sale in newsagents around town. It was different from other magazines and newspapers because it was small and printed on thin, bleached paper. When you opened the pages it felt dry and brittle as if it would crumble to dust if you rubbed it between your fingers.

I read *Rap* most months. It reflected back a different version of Rochdale than the *Rochdale Observer*. The stories were about the town's mill owners, MPs, council officials, councillors, solicitors, doctors, landowners, Rotarians, Masons and, later, a Rochdale AFC stalwart. These were stalked with gleeful relish, especially Cyril Smith, Rochdale's famously rotund MP. As they saw it he was a serpent forming a protective ring around a conspiracy of self-interest and nepotism, no less.

Smith was lampooned in a comic strip called *Fatman*. Rog Dale (*Fatman's* 'real' name) was shy and timid. While he tucks into his dinner of cows' udders and black peas, he grumbles to his mother that, unlike Gracie Fields, he'll never become famous. 'You will be, our kid,' she reassures. Later that day he rubs a magic clog-iron and turns into *Fatman,* taking to the skies in a cape.

My mum liked Cyril Smith. Most mums did because he'd 'put Rochdale on the map.' She had seen him shopping at the market and he was jolly and friendly with everyone.

"I wish they'd just leave him alone. Why does everyone have a go at him?"

When dad came across a copy of *Rap* while out on a job he had a quick read but I think, similar to most Rochdale people, he felt buying his own would make him unclean somehow. It printed home addresses, telephone numbers and photographs of houses belonging to the wealthy and powerful in the town. One front cover had pictures of property belonging to the town's estate agents. Dad shook his head:

"I can't believe they get away with this."

I dreaded the thought of Rochdale losing their League status. I knew instinctively that this was our indisputable mark of distinction. We were members of the oldest league in the world, the same exclusive club that had Manchester United and Liverpool et al among its number. Despite the woeful seasons and ignominious defeats we had remained in this hierarchy for fifty years.

My life had become conjoined to the heartbeat of the club. This included the turn of the seasons. In summer we arrived in shirtsleeves, thin jackets draped over our arms. The air had the tang of cut grass and optimism. The trees behind the Sandy Lane End were thick and green. Sunlight danced across the pitch, silhouettes spilling everywhere.

Autumn brought fog, drizzle and a shiver as we began the inevitable slip down the league. Bonfires burned in back gardens and on distant hills in early November. Volunteers shovelled snow into a thick buttress of white around the pitch in January. The dusty snow that remained was drawn intermittently into small clouds and sent spinning around the players. In the stands, cups of coffee were held tightly in cold hands.

Cyril Smith, without magic clog-iron.

The rain still came down in March and April but it was lighter. Sometimes the sun splintered the raindrops into shards of Technicolor light. We might score at this surreal moment and it felt otherworldly, as if we were watching ourselves watching our team score.

At the final games of the season, early in May, jackets were back across arms, the warm air wafting through the stands. Leaves had returned to the trees. People living nearby leaned on their garden gates as we passed. Kids played in the driveway, little girls skittering along in their mam's shoes, the family dog reclining in the sunshine. The pitch was dry and hard, the ball bouncing unevenly, the players hurrying to the touchline for bottles of water. Another year gone.

Rochdale made an ominous signing in the close season. Phil Ashworth, who had been top scorer with both Workington and Southport when they lost their League status in consecutive seasons, was brought in by Mike Ferguson.

They began the new season as they had finished the last, taking fourteen games to record a win. During this run Wigan Athletic, with a certain predictability, recorded their first ever League win, beating Rochdale 3–0 in September. At least the away form had improved, slightly. The 0–0 draw at Newport County was their first away clean sheet in thirty-two matches.

The draw for the first round of the FA Cup was again unkind. Football League opposition would have granted the club a routine and inconspicuous exit (few countenanced the possibility of a win) but we were pitched against Droylsden of the Cheshire League.

We lost 1–0 and had been knocked out of the cup for the third consecutive season by a team made up of amateur footballers.

"We had no character, no pride, no nothing," said Ferguson.

Simon Roberts' dad was a member of the Labour party and the only person I knew who had *Rap* on order. I told him I sometimes bought it, usually from Finnerty's newsagents in town. He turned in his chair to face me and reached down for the magazine on the coffee table. He waved it as he spoke.

"All this stuff about bosses and what they're paid and what they're up to, *that's* interesting and something we want to know about. This other stuff, it just puts people off."

I must have looked puzzled. He sighed:

"You know, all this in here about giving grants to queers so they can open centres all over the shop. We don't want to read about *that*. It gets people's back's up. Does no good at all. Piffle. And have you read this letter* here? Fancy carrying a bloody letter like that."

It was from the Rochdale Women's Liberation Group which had taken offence to an advert in the paper for *Sauna*

* I've kept the issue containing the letter. There is no better résumé of those crazy politically correct times.

Corner in Yorkshire Street where women were offered, among other treatments, eyebrow shaping for 50p, eyelash dying for the same price and a 'skin peel' for £1. The group claimed it 'taught women to be ashamed of their bodies.'

Mr Roberts shook his head.

"What a load of cat arse."

By Christmas Rochdale had only ten points and were second from bottom. Mike Ferguson was sacked and Doug Collins, a former Burnley player, was appointed player/manager. He told the press, using all his powers of circumlocution:

"My aim will be to put, as you might say, a new coat of paint on the name of Rochdale AFC. In some circles people might have tried to make Rochdale a bit of a joke lately. I intend to take away any possibility of such a word being mentioned in the same breath as Rochdale. The task is formidable."

It was possible to sense his eagerness from the photographs. He looked ready to climb out of the frame and busy himself answering the phone, pulling on a jacket, dashing to his car. He had to remain patient because Rochdale, like the rest of Britain, was under snow. Motorists were stranded on the M62 and snowdrifts reached seven feet high in Wardle. Three months passed without a home match.

In March, when Spotland thawed and football returned, Collins was to oversee a feat that verged on the miraculous.

I engineered a scheme to get myself a free ticket for a Rochdale home match. I don't know why I did this; I had reasonable pocket money and wages from my paper round so there was no need to resort to such craven duplicity.

Down the seasons I had noted the name 'Alex McGregor' in the Aldershot team. I didn't know what he looked like or what position he played. I just liked the sound of his name—the syllables crashing together like cymbals.

A few days before we were due to play Aldershot I wrote and informed him that he was my favourite player in the division. I'd love to see him play against Rochdale, but, alas, my mum and dad couldn't afford to buy me a ticket. I received a reply by return of post. He was, 'delighted to hear from me and learn that I admired his style of play'. He said he would leave two tickets at the reception desk at Spotland ('One for you and one for your old man'). He also said the envelope would contain passes for the players' lounge. We could have a drink together after the match. He promised me a glass of lemonade.

We left it until close to kick-off time before collecting the tickets. We feared McGregor, possibly in his playing strip, might lurk near the office ready to shake our hands and show excessive gratitude to his two biggest fans.

The game was spoiled by our dread that the Tannoy man would announce our names and remind us that we were due to meet up with McGregor afterwards. At the final whistle we quickly headed home. I was still apprehensive: McGregor had our address. He might have been concerned that I had fallen ill after the game and been unable to meet him in the lounge. I went straight to bed, listening for a coach pulling up at the bottom of our drive and a pair of footsteps growing louder as they reached the front door.

"Is your lad in? He was supposed to meet me tonight."

Doug Collins galvanised a run of form that surpassed anything the club had achieved before. In the previous season they had taken forty-four matches to record seven wins. At the close of 1978/79 they won seven out of their last eight games.

The most outstanding result was a 3–0 win at Barnsley who had been in the promotion race all season and were expected to beat their visitors soundly. Les Barlow, the sports reporter covering the club's fortunes for the *Rochdale Observer*, was known for his taut, pragmatic prose but the win caught him uncharacteristically giddy. Under the headline 'Magnificent Magical Rochdale' he wrote: 'This win will go down as one of the best ever scored by a Rochdale team in the history of the club.'

The battle to avoid a re-election application depended on Rochdale securing a point in the final game at Crewe Alexandra. They won 2–1.

I had scrapbooks and spiral-bound folders in which I stored my cuttings and artefacts but my correspondence with Mountford and other players was kept in a special place: a small padded box with a gold clasp. The lid was veined and the interior covered in soft cherry-coloured cloth. It was like a jewellery box without the revolving fairy on top.

A few years after these letters had been lovingly stored away, I left my then-girlfriend waiting in my bedroom while I had a bath. She noticed a half-open drawer with the box inside and thought she had discovered a collection of beautifully-framed love letters. She gave in to temptation. The first she found was Mountford's, the one wrapped in dainty pink tissue. She read, among others, my communication with David Jackson, Buckie Thistle's moustachioed centre-forward, and perused Terry Gennoe's list of his ten best ever saves.

As I flounced into the room, drying my hair and whistling, she retched the word from her lips:

"Weirdo."

If Rochdale had been beaten by Crewe they would almost certainly have lost their League status. The club was aware that the goodwill that had seen them regularly re-elected could not last indefinitely. Chairman Fred Ratcliffe had garnered much of this support through force of personality.

I learned of Fred's significance soon after I first attended Spotland. Fans talked about him with great affection. He was known as 'Little Freddie' because he stood at was just over five feet. He was often pictured in the *Rochdale Observer*. In a row of gleaming faces and dinner suits at a sportsmen's dinner, Fred was at shoulder height, round-faced, head sat deep in his shoulders, eyes bleached out behind wire-rimmed glasses. The tide had washed him up among all these tall, handsome people and he looked uneasy, as if he'd prefer to be somewhere else. Spotland, probably.

He was managing director of FS Ratcliffe Springs and for thirty-two years had redirected a sizeable portion of its profits into the football club. Conditions at his works were austere, similar to many others in Rochdale. The hours were long and the pay low. Many of the 320 staff resented Fred because he drove a Rolls Royce and dressed in expensive sheepskin coats. He was often in the proximity of attractive women, invariably much younger than himself, and his attachment to Rochdale AFC and various football bodies gave him social standing, allowing him to mix with famous players and managers. These factors along with his millionaire status and reported income of almost £600 per week made him of special interest to *Rap*.

A great aunty died and while we were clearing out her house dad had an idea for a family business. We'd set ourselves up as market traders, using her stuff to get us started; it's what she would have wanted.

He rented a stall on the flea market for a month of Wednesdays. It was July and me and my sister could help because we were off school.

After setting up for the first time I wandered down a few aisles and came across an oil painting of an oriental-looking man sitting on a jetty.

"Excuse me, how much is this?"

"Fifty," replied the woman stallholder.

Fred Ratcliffe, Spotland saviour.

It seemed quite expensive considering it wasn't framed and had been jammed in a large wooden box with other pictures. She shouted across:

"I can't go any lower than 50p, love."

Over the course of a week *Rap*'s reporters trailed Freddie Ratcliffe as part of a 'special investigation'. They discovered that after attending a match at Spotland he visited the Hare and Hounds pub in Bury Road, Rochdale, where 'he sat apart from others, with a blonde woman, aged close to forty, who stood close to the stool on which he was sat. The relationship seemed close as she snuggled up to him often and they whispered together'.

The next day, at another bar, 'Ratcliffe reappeared with his female companion of the previous night (now known to be called Marjorie). She looked after him, pouring out his drinks, cuddling close and making him laugh.' They noted that, 'Fred is not, anywhere we saw him, the centre or soul of the party.'

The rest of Fred's week comprised visits to pubs, hotels, restaurants, football matches and sportsmen's dinners, usually in the company of Marjorie. His wife Florence was apparently back at their palatial home set in its own grounds above Rochdale.

Rap joyfully and meticulously condensed his week: he was at the engineering works for thirteen hours and thirty-three minutes; he spent twenty-four hours in pubs; thirty hours at hotel bars; and his average lunchtime alcohol intake was three halves of bitter and three whisky chasers.

He also had a cocktail bar in his office. *Rap*, in a solitary concession to benevolence, commented: 'He clearly cares deeply and is prepared to put his money where his mouth is, about saving Rochdale Football Club.'

The two page feature closed: 'We don't envy him. But we do oppose the system which allows such excesses for the privileged few.'

The astounding re-election escape lifted hope to a new level. Rochdale AFC appeared to be reinventing itself and confirmation came with the first signing of the close season. Alan Weir, the former captain of England's youth team, left Sunderland where first-team opportunities were limited and chose to launch his career at Rochdale.

We had signed one of the best young footballers in the country and, like all the top players, he had a perm. Catching the mood,*The Razor's Edge*, a barber's shop in Rochdale, began advertising in the match programme. A 'curly perm' was £10.50 and a 'shaggy look' £14.50.

Rochdale's next signing was Dennis Wann from Darlington. He was older than Weir with thinner hair but could still sustain a perm. We meant business.

The pre-season friendlies included a home match against Den Bosch of Holland's first division. We viewed this as new found sophistication and stared incredulously at a team sheet containing the names Diet Kamps, Nol Van de Proot, Tonnie Kanters and Peter Paarloos.

Fred and Marjorie made the cover of *Rap*, so there was little chance of anyone in Rochdale missing the story. The episode undoubtedly raised a belly laugh on the shop floor of the spring works but probably enhanced his raffish notoriety among football friends. His lifestyle was, after all, hardly atypical of the wealthy, small-town, self-made men who invariably ran football clubs. He was, to them, a 'character', a peculiarly robust little man. Once you'd met him you didn't forget him or his football club. Supporters, meanwhile, were largely unconcerned about his infidelity and extravagance. They wondered why the people at *Rap* had given up a week of their lives to discover what everyone already knew. Besides, Freddie was a Rochdale fan; he could do what he liked.

On a still and warm summer night Rochdale beat Den Bosch 7–2. They played football that was authentically *breathtaking*. Every player had the game of his life. It was football as poetry, the ball passed exquisitely to feet and falling under control as if by magic. Dennis Wann, for example, received a pass at his midriff and nonchalantly adjusted his weight to send the ball on a direct route to the top of the net. He walked back to the half-way line brushing off the congratulations of his team-mates: it was nothing, he was an artist.

Afterwards Les Barlow seemed to be understating when he gushed in the *Rochdale Observer*: 'Promotion is a naughty word with some at Spotland, but the truth is that few Fourth Division teams will be able to live with Dale if

rap 56

monthly

Rochdale's Alternative Paper

MARCH 1977 7ᵖ

RAP SPIES ON

RATCLIFFE

they produce this sort of form.' Doug Collins issued a small note of caution:

"It's almost frightening to say it but we were brilliant. It worries me that everything should go so well."

I O

Nudes in the Grass

THE MARKET WAS POPULATED BY PEOPLE YOU DIDN'T realise existed any more or hadn't noticed because they didn't usually gather in one place. Old ladies, who, between stalls, seemed hardly able to walk, picked their way vigorously through mounds of second hand shoes, some tied together as pairs but mostly loose.

"Got the other one to this?" they'd ask.

"Somewhere in there. You'll have to take a look."

"I have taken a bloody look."

Blokes flocked around tool stalls, thumbing their way through trays of pliers and screwdrivers.

"How much is this?"

"One pound fifty, it's practically new."

"It's got some rust on it, look."

The trader took it from him and rubbed it with his thumb:

"It hasn't now."

We soon pondered on Den Bosch. Blackpool, admittedly of a higher division, knocked us out of the League Cup and Bournemouth beat us 2–0 on the opening day of the season. By the time we travelled to Halifax Town in mid-September and lost 1–0 it was manifest that we were as woeful as ever. We had won once in the season's first seven matches.

The game at Halifax was played on a drizzly Tuesday night. It was the end of summer and the end of a surge of hope that had briefly engulfed the town. I went there by train; dad couldn't make it, he was working late. When supporters reached the station at Halifax after the match, the disappointment and bitterness fermented into anger. We were herded on to the platform and kept there by a line of barking police dogs. The chanting was loud and coarse. Fans pushed forward, some at the front goading police and managing to break through and seek out rival fans for one-on-one fights.

I saw older lads from school, many of them drunk. One asked me to jump down on the tracks and pass him handfuls of stones to throw at the police. I said it was too dangerous.

The train arrived and we clambered aboard noisily. I sat down facing two girls who had left my school a few years before. They seemed to be the only girls among the Rochdale fans. One of them was called Maggie. She had dark brown eyes picked out in smudgy eye-liner. Throughout the train I could hear smashing and shouting. A lad staggered in, pushing open the doors roughly:

"They're knocking fuck out of the carriage in front.

They're trying to get the toilet out of the window."
Everyone laughed.

The train was being systematically destroyed, coming apart beneath kicks and blows. Ripped up seats, fire extinguishers and sinks flashed by the window. Maggie's boyfriend stood in the aisle, frequently leaving for a few minutes, returning red-faced and kissing her crudely on the lips. She'd break off from the conversation with her friend as he gripped the back of her head tightly and held her face against his.

The train was halted at Hebden Bridge and almost 100 Rochdale fans were taken back to Halifax where they were interviewed by police throughout the night about the damage.

Word must have got around that we were new because the stall was soon surrounded. Luckily we backed on to Wally's pitch and he had done the markets for years. He wore checked trousers and was quick on his feet for a man in his early sixties.

He put us straight: we had no right to be pleased with ourselves because we were practically giving stuff away. We had to wise up, he said, otherwise they'd make mugs of us. He warned us gravely about *the Paki's*. They wouldn't pay what you wanted. They'd barter, except they wouldn't barter fairly. They'd stand there saying, '5p, I give you 5p' over and over again until you were blue in the face and finally sold it to them for 5p just to be rid of the buggers.

"I'm telling you now: don't barter with a Paki. You'll

only lose. It's in their culture see, to take the piss."

Nothing got past Wally. He could see everything at once. He kept a watch on his own stall and looked out for us too. We wondered how he made a living because he sold things that either had a highly specific use or looked as if they had come from a skip. He had torn lampshades; shoes with their soles hanging off; Halloween masks (in summer?); keep-fit LPs (scratched with ripped sleeves); out-of-date guide books to the outer Hebrides; cassette tapes of Israeli folk songs; washed-out T-shirts; Action Men with arms or legs missing; sun bleached colour-by-numbers paintings.

Above his stall was a guitar suspended on a piece of string. The body was dinted and flakes of wood had broken through the veneer. It was like a motif for his business and had a sticker on it: 'NFS.' No one knew what the letters stood for. Several times through the day, people asked:

"How much is the guitar, mate?"

Wally shook his head slowly.

"Not for sale."

"Well why is it on your stall then?"

He didn't have time to discuss the matter. He'd told them already.

"Not for sale," he'd say in exactly the same tone as before. He'd stand perfectly still, hands welded to his cardigan pockets. When they had moved on, muttering, he'd turn to my dad:

"How many times do I have to tell them? How many times?"

Four days after the Halifax game we played Portsmouth at home. I was reading the programme before kick-off when I saw my name in it. A few weeks earlier I had entered a competition where schoolboys were asked to write a match report. My piece on the Rochdale v Walsall match where I had called Alan Buckley a 'pint-sized striker' had won.

After the initial surge of excitement I was flustered: what if someone from school found out? No one wrote out of choice, it was something you were made to do for homework. It would be viewed with the same disdain had I won a sewing or cookery competition. Wasn't it also showing off — to have your name in print like that? Who did I think I was?

I had almost forgotten I had entered the competition because, by now, at the age of fifteen, I was already pretty much a full-time writer. I was still producing programmes for the games I played in — or didn't, if Smithies had dropped me — and this took up most evenings. I set myself deadlines and couldn't sleep if I was behind schedule. I did them on a huge Underwood typewriter my dad had cadged from an office where he had been working.

After recovering from the shock of Mountford's departure I had also resumed the scrapbooks. This was time-consuming, especially as I had hit upon a rich source of material. I collected newspapers and magazines from people on our estate, piling them up in an old pram as I went door to door. I checked through them for mentions of Rochdale and most weeks I had the match report from every daily newspaper. When the garage was full, dad rang a paper merchant and he collected them. We used the money to buy new kits or balls* for the team.

We let Wally down. We sold things. Dad was too shy to barter properly. When the old folk shuffled up, their feet too swollen to fit their shoes anymore, their clothes tatty, he wanted to give away the coats and jumpers for free. These were people from fifty years before, left behind, grabbing at cast-offs, desperate for a bargain, knocking dried mud from second hand shoes against the market wall. I think it reminded mum and dad of when they were kids. They had grown up among people like this, when you were posh if you had an inside toilet and enough decent clothes to walk the streets on Whit Sunday.

The old ladies would rummage through the clothes, asking how much everything was, and mum — standing at the side — would whisper:

"Let her have it, just give it to her."

Mum usually secreted herself among the dresses hanging down from a wooden beam and only moved to the centre of the stall if it was unavoidable. Customers were surprised to hear a voice from the wings:

"It's a size 14, that."

---

* Footballs used to be very expensive. My dad still can't believe he can see a cage of balls in Aldi or wherever and they cost a quarter of what they did back in the late 1970s. He sometimes buys them for his grandsons (who already have more than enough) merely because he can afford to.

They'd scan across and see her shadowy figure. Mum was worried in case she was spotted by anyone who knew her. She was embarrassed that the family had 'come to this.' She believed you worked hard and saved so you didn't have to buy second hand things. Selling them was even worse.

Within a few weeks we had sold or given away the stock and hardly broke even.

Doug Collins had been considered a deity in the summer but months later his nobility had waned substantially. Rochdale won twice in the opening twenty matches of the 1979/80 season. The earlier optimism served to hone the swamp-deep disappointment.

Fans wrote letters to the *Rochdale Observer*: 'Deplorable rubbish'; 'Rochdale claiming to be a football team is a breach of the Trade Descriptions Act'; 'A disgrace, shameful and disgusting'; and, finally, 'I implore Mr Collins to take up the surgeon's knife and cut away until the Dale are cleaned.'

A major source of discontent was Collins' reluctance to select himself for the team. During his time at the club he began just six games. He was player/manager but was perceived as doing only half the job. He made his case valiantly:

"How can a chap be fit to play when he has the cares of the world on his shoulders, when he misses sleep because of poor results and when he's so pre-occupied with management that he cannot get the right mental fitness to play football?"

The final whistle, another home defeat.

A few of us were invited to a party. Well, we'd heard about it and we knew the lad who was having it and he kind of, sort of liked us, we thought, probably.

We made our way through the streets with carrier bags full of home-brew that tasted like cold ox-tail soup. We didn't need to know the house number or the street: we'd hear the noise. We'd had a few decent swigs before setting off so were already laughing, breaking off to slash in the bushes or down an entry. We found the house but it took a while to attract someone's attention and get them to answer the door.

Kids were everywhere—in the front room, sitting on the sideboard and the hi-fi unit; in the hallway kicking a small plastic football around; on the stairs, moving sullenly to the side when anyone passed; and in the bedrooms, jumping on the bed or laughing at wedding photographs they'd found in a drawer. Only the girls and sixth-formers had pooled their drinks, plonking them on a table in the kitchen. The rest kept their supply within sight, feeling constantly for the plastic bag at their feet, slapping down the odd sly hand.

I was new to drink, at fifteen, and soon in a formless new world. Girls were easy to speak to now and you could be cheeky and tease them, saying things aloud that used to be just thoughts. A lad was throwing up in the sink, holding on to the sides, his knees buckling with every wretch. His mate, giggling, picked up a bottle and hit him hard on the back of the head. The bottle bounced off and landed on the floor.

On my way to the toilet a lad accidentally bumped into me on the stairs. I'd seen him around school. He was younger than me.

"Watch it," I snapped.

"I'm really sorry," he said.

He was level with me. I could see fear in his eyes.

"Just don't do it again, okay?"

"No, I won't. It was an accident, I was just trying to pass," he blurted.

I grabbed him by the shirt and drew my face close to his. "I'm warning you."

I'd heard this kind of pathetic reproach said by others; it was strange hearing myself say it. I came back down the stairs a few minutes later and the lad was sitting cowed on the edge of the settee. I motioned with my head and he nodded back, looking down at the carpet. I had been under the impression that anything you did when you were drunk was locked into a dream; it didn't really happen. I apologised. He said he wasn't bothered, it didn't matter. He was very talkative.

"I should have looked where I was going really."

"No, I shouldn't have done it."

He was very grown-up about it for a 13-year-old:

"It's okay, really. Most of us get carried away when we've had a drink."

He left soon afterwards, making a point of touching me on the arm as he passed and saying there were no hard feelings. His benevolence made me feel even worse.

Doug Collins was sacked in November 1979 after holding the position for eleven months.

"Whoever gets my job has got it made. If only they had been more patient, I would have given them what they wanted."

One reporter saw his dismissal as symptomatic of sport's new ruthlessness. Peter Thomas wrote in the *Daily Mail*: 'Doug Collins has gone 'shocked and staggered' and so am I; but I'm not surprised because heroes don't last long even in Rochdale nowadays. Rochdale will never be the same again and, insignificant though it may be, somehow neither will soccer."

Collins' final piece of business had been to sign the striker Jimmy Seal from Darlington. He was viewed as the final addition to Rochdale's travelling circus. They were now, ladies and gentlemen, boys and girls, ten clowns and a performing Seal.

In the school holidays and on Sundays dad took me on jobs with him to mills, offices or factories — places that had to be closed to carry out the work.

I liked exploring these empty buildings but dad didn't want me rooting and was apprehensive about my leaving the site where he was working. I'd read the notices pinned to the walls and check on the postcards and pin-ups near the lathes. There was often a drinks machine in the corridor.

"Fancy a cup of tea, dad?"

I usually had hot chocolate, feeding in the coin and hearing its insides shunt into life as if taken by surprise.

I imagined the noise on a weekday, the machines thundering and people having to shout above the din. I took books along to read and dad didn't mind; I was never much use at practical things. I read *Animal Farm* in one of the biggest factories in Lancashire; very apt.

Doug Collins was replaced by Bob Stokoe, a man who was part of FA Cup folklore. At the final whistle of the 1973 cup final, after his Sunderland team had beaten Leeds United 1–0, he raced across the Wembley turf in a cream-coloured raincoat and trilby hat to embrace goalkeeper, Jim Montgomery.

The press was invited to his first training session at Rochdale. The trilby had been replaced with a bobble hat, the suit by a loose fitting tracksuit. He was still lean at 48-years-old, posing with the squad, hands behind his back, broad smile on his face. A long line of players stood by his side, some with their arms crossed, others staring down at the floor. They looked as if they had been transplanted from a boys' comic, a collection of misfits and misshapes rounded up from all corners of town to make up the numbers in an impromptu football competition. They each wore different clothes: stripes, jeans, rugby jerseys, T-shirts, tracksuit tops with broken zips, tight shorts, long shorts, slack shorts, short shorts. Physically they were all different to one another too. Bobby Scaife had legs like oil drums, a big pirate's face and straggly beard. Ted Oliver was as thin as the goal-line and almost as white. David Esser, the human tree stump. Eric Snookes' red face and red hair burned bright in the fading light of a late-autumn after-noon. Alan Weir's perm had collapsed. Make of these what you will, Mr Stokoe, and, incidentally, that's your lot: there's no money available for new signings.

Rochdale was Stokoe's ninth managerial appointment and the third club he had managed on two separate occasions. He had started the season at Blackpool but left on a 'point of principle'. His resignation as Sunderland manager had been on a similar issue.

We'd been working in the town centre and I was helping dad load the van. He caught sight of *Nudes in the Grass* and began chuckling.

"He wants locking up, doesn't he?"

Rochdale's 'town artist', Michael Dames, had borrowed a paint-laying contraption, the type used to mark out foot-ball pitches probably, and drawn two huge nude figures embracing on the steep hillside behind the town hall.

Dames was employed by Rochdale Council which meant — as the *Rochdale Observer* reminded everyone glee-fully — his wages came out of 'rate-payers' pockets'.

His first piece had been *European Unity Emergency Ward*, a tree trunk placed on a bed with bandages wrapped around its branches. The trunk was covered with a satin bedspread which had a map of Europe stitched into the cloth. At the bottom of the bed he hung a sign: 'Kiss a Foreigner Today.'

"The bandages on the off-shoots are meant to represent countries in Europe which at sometime through history have been damaged by war," he explained. "The boundaries between the countries should dissolve and, like the sea, become one."

Letter-writers to the *Rochdale Observer* were livid. He wasn't an *artist*. Anyone could put a tree in bed and wrap bandages around it. The council was funding a lefty indulgence. They should reclassify the job as 'town comedian' and have done with it. One of dad's friends said: "What did they call him, town artist? Town piss artist, more like."

11

Bread Roll Christ

ROCHDALE SENT ME A PAIR OF MATCH TICKETS AS A prize for winning the writing competition. I wrote a note of thanks and asked whether I could help with the programme. I received a reply from a man called Jack Hammill who told me he was a freelance journalist and did the programme as a favour to the club. He invited me to attend a match and sit with him in the press box.

My legs fell heavy as I walked towards the officials' entrance at the next match. My mouth was dry and I had to check that my voice hadn't evaporated. I wanted to skirt the door and carry on walking around the ground. My ambition to become a journalist suddenly felt vain and pointless. Who was I to go through that door? On the other side were people taller and broader and cleverer than me; I didn't have a map of their world.

I told the commissionaire I had been asked to report to Jack Hammill.

"He's not here yet."

I asked if I could wait by the door.

"If you like."

People collected guest tickets in manilla envelopes from the club office and showed them to the commissionaire. They were well-dressed in long black coats with shirt and ties underneath. The women wore dresses and high-heels, and smelled of perfume. They were fussed over, guided through the door. They joked with the commissionaire, telling him he was looking smart today. He smiled and made a show of rubbing his lapels. When they saw someone they knew also receiving an envelope, they shouted over.

"What's in there, a bribe for the ref?"

They noticed me by the door and one or two winked playfully.

"Alright son?"

I nodded.

After a few minutes the commissionaire told me Jack had arrived. I saw him from the back: a thin figure in an anorak tied tightly at the waist. He joked with the girl at the ticket office. As he turned towards the entrance, he saw two or three more people he knew. They shook his hand, one gripped his forearm. Jack's movements were quick and sharp. While he spoke he looked past these people and lifted his hand to acknowledge others. Although he was about sixty, he had extremely thick hair. He regularly scooped it from the front of his head and pushed it back. A notebook was jammed into his pocket and he kept pulling it out and putting it back again as if signalling that he had to go; he had a job to do.

"This young man's been waiting for you Jack," said the commissionaire.

"Come on, I'll show you where the press box is," said Jack.

It was dark on the other side of the entrance and it took a few seconds for my eyes to adjust. We were beneath the Main Stand in a wide corridor lined with doors. A glow of white light was visible at the end when the swing-doors opened and the pitch became visible.

The thoroughfare was busy. Middle-aged men in tracksuits dodged among the ladies in white blouses carrying trays of small triangular sandwiches A small notice on one door read 'Home' and next to it was another: 'Visitors'. A net was propped against the entrance to the changing rooms containing four or five footballs.

A huddle of people had gathered around the door closest to the pitch. Jack told me it was the tea room and I could go in at half-time and have tea and biscuits if I liked. I peered in as we passed. The room was thick with smoke. People were close together, talking and eating food from paper plates as if they were at a wedding buffet.

The press box was at the top of a short flight of steep stairs. It was a small area cut into the stand and contained five or six benches and narrow planks of wood that served as tables. There was barely enough room to shuffle down the 'aisles' and sit at a bench. Jack asked me to go in first and followed me in. He began clawing at the phones scattered around.

"That's knackered," he announced. "And this has never bloody worked."

He found one he was happy with and passed me the wire that ran out of the back.

"Here, you're younger than me. Bend down and put that

in the socket will you? It's under your legs somewhere."

I had to reposition myself to find enough room to lean forwards. I found the socket; it had worked loose and was rocking on two screws.

"Right, we need one for you now. Try this."

He slammed a phone in front of me and I lifted the receiver. Its wire was draped over the bench and snaked down into the darkness. I could hear the dialling tone. I was set.

Jack told me he covered Rochdale's matches for lots of newspapers, and radio and television stations. At half-time and full-time he relayed the score to the BBC and ITV. He provided goal-flashes too, ringing over the scorer's name and the time of the goal. He also did 'runners' where, every few minutes, he phoned over a block of copy to the *Football Pink* or *Radio Manchester*. Most of the reports were short — the *Daily Mirror* might order sixty words, the *Sunday People* a hundred, but collectively it was a great deal of work.

"You'll soon get the hang of it," he said.

I was feet away from dad who was sitting on the other side of a wooden partition in the stand. Before the game he had said he wouldn't talk to me or acknowledge that he knew me in case it 'embarrassed' me.

When he had first arrived in Rochdale our 'town artist' described it as 'a go-ahead place with a reputation for pioneering.' Michael Dames was referring to the Rochdale Pioneers, the founders of the co-operative movement.

Hammill, Rochdale.

Their small shop in Toad Lane had been a place of pilgrimage for people from all over the world, though it was now sandwiched between the service area of the new shopping precinct and a busy dual carriageway. Unknown to Dames, Rochdale had done with pioneering.

When he was called upon to defend his work in the *Rochdale Observer* the paper usually included his picture; the same one every time. He wore the expression of someone who had never seen a camera before. He looked right through it, forgetting to smile or hold himself upright. He had his hands in his pockets, his shirt lap ruffled at the waist. He looked as if he was soft-shoeing across the pavement outside Tesco while he waited for his wife to do the weekly shopping.

The tree trunk had been displayed in Rochdale Art Gallery. He realised that if he really wanted to stab at the conservative heart of the town he needed to accost them at bus stops or while they were shopping. So, he chopped up discarded telegraph poles, hammered them into the ground and scratched silly faces on them. And, for his final trick, he painstakingly moulded fibreglass loaves of bread and arranged them into the shape of a figure. His *Bread Roll Christ* was mounted on a wall at the rear of the Arndale Centre in Middleton.* This was his goodbye to Rochdale.

---

* In the autumn of 2006 I visited Middleton Library in search of photographs for this book. I found one of *Bread Roll Christ* and on the back someone had written: 'Breadman Christ sculpture by Michael Dames mounted on Middleton Way gable of the Arndale Centre. Erected May 1980, removed April 1984, due to vandalism and general public dislike.'

I foisted myself upon Jack and began working with him on a regular basis in the press box. He gave me a list of numbers, the times I had to ring and how many words they each wanted.

I was afraid of being overheard and spoke quietly. The copy-takers couldn't hear me. They were under pressure:

"You'll have to speak up. Didn't catch any of that, son."

After a while I began to shout. If you didn't, the job didn't get done.

National newspapers sporadically sent along their own reporters, so there was sometimes up to ten of us in there, yelling and shouting, and fighting for handsets and phone lines. The chatter became furious after a goal was scored. Fans leaned over and shouted:

"Calm down lads. You'll all have bloody heart attacks."

The supporters were so close they could hear copy being dictated. They would wait until a phone was put down and rise from their seats.

"And that was a load of balls you've just told them."

No one in the box dared to divert their gaze from the pitch.

"Hey, you. You know very well who I'm talking to. I'm over here, Ginger."

They'd always find a nickname for the person they wanted. The press box's sole ginger-haired occupant acknowledged the cries. The rest of us could relax.

"What's all that crap what you've just been saying there? We've bloody hammered you today and you've scored a lucky goal. That's all, a lucky bloody goal."

It was always assumed journalists supported the clubs they reported on. Fans' comments were usually laughed off but reporters sometimes joined in the banter:

"Lucky goals win matches, my friend."

"You haven't bloody won yet."

On this occasion Rochdale rallied and recorded a rare win, 3–1. The supporter rose from his seat after each goal and mocked:

"What's the score now, *my friend*?"

Before the end of the match up to a dozen fans were asking this and mimicking the reporter's accent whenever he used the phone. He was from 'down South'. They asked him if he was getting a bit cold, all this way up north and whether his mam had dressed him properly that morning, in his vest and everything.

Rochdale were still losing, often heavily. Huddersfield Town beat us 5–1. A month later we lost to Tranmere Rovers by the same score. Bob Stokoe was so incensed he fined each player half a week's wages, reportedly £35. The Professional Footballers' Association (PFA) challenged the decision but Stokoe was adamant:

"I demanded 100 per cent effort from my players and I didn't get it. It was my most embarrassing moment in football for many years."

Stokoe was supported by a Rochdale fan calling himself 'Nevermissamatch' who wrote in the *Rochdale Observer*: 'The players appeared determined not to play—almost as though there was a conspiracy. The fans who travelled to Tranmere were cheated.'

Jack was a wily operator. He had his own designated phone line at Spotland and protected his domain. You didn't sit on *his* bench. If anyone dared, they soon knew about it.

"That seat's taken, son."

A young reporter in his best suit, a long way from home turf, would rise dutifully, picking up his stopwatch, three pens, spiral bound notebook, Mars bar, can of pop, match programme, team-sheet and list of statistics.

"You might find some room at the back."

When Jack answered the phone, he said:

"Hammill, Rochdale" as if we had our own suite staffed by scores of reporters.

I stole phrases from Jack and others around me. If they had a striker *charging* through a defence, I had him *dashing*; *sloppy* defending became *slack* marking.

In the haze of broken phones and looming deadlines, knocked over cups of coffee, hard-of-hearing copy girls and blokes in overcoats blocking your view, the game was invariably lost. We recorded every detail of matches we'd not actually watched.

Kids turned up from all over town for Tina Jenkins' party. Among them was a group of gatecrashers with thin, mean faces who were looking about themselves furtively, sharing whispered jokes. When they danced, they infringed on people's space, daring them to respond. One was wearing a Hawaiian shirt and stretch jeans with a white belt at his waist hanging loose at the front. He had a patchy moustache and his head slumped into his shoulders like a crow sitting on a fence. Tina's family—her gran, younger sister, and mum and dad—stared down from a large photograph on the wall. They were standing in front of a painted backdrop of a bookcase, her dad's hands on her mum's shoulders.

A few of us left on the pretext of calling at the off licence; we knew what was going to happen next. When we got back kids were crying and whimpering all through the house. The phone had been ripped from the wall, pictures were smashed on the floor, the coffee table was tipped over. Some of the girls were hysterical. One or two were dabbing cuts with their shirt-cuffs in the kitchen. The police were on their way and Tina's parents had been contacted at the pub.

Tina was sitting at the bottom of the stairs, sobbing loudly. She spoke in short gusts:

"My mum and dad. Are going to kill. Me. When. They. Get. Here."

While she was hugged and reassured, people tidied up. She'd break off from crying to tell someone where the bin-liners were kept or the dust pan and brush. The shattered glass was swept up and photographs put back in their approximate places. Two lads used a wooden mallet to straighten the legs on the broken coffee table. All this was done drunkenly with people struggling to stay upright as they straightened piles of records or repositioned ornaments. While they went about their business, they brooded:

"Why do they do it? Why do people do things like this?"

Tina's parents arrived. Before she could explain, her dad held out his arms and clasped her. She cried even louder. She was much shorter than him and he was able to look over her shoulder while they embraced. We were embarrassed to witness this private moment and stared at the floor. When they separated, Mr Jenkins stepped gingerly into the room, followed by his wife. He was a big bloke with black hair and a moustache but she was tiny and moved skittishly like a bird. The phone that had been torn from the wall was now placed on the table with its cord wrapped neatly around it. Shards of glass had been swept from the carpet. The curtains were back on the rails. Tina followed them, a few feet behind.

"I'm sorry dad, really sorry."

"It wasn't your fault love."

As he walked through to the kitchen, he was on guard.

"Are they still around?"

"No, they've all gone."

"Are you sure? Do you know everyone here?"

She said she did and began crying again. She told him how everyone had helped clean up and how she was lucky to have such good friends. While he listened, he scanned the room, nodding to us. He gave a short speech:

"I'd like to thank you all for helping out. Me and Tina's mum were worried about what we were going to find when we got back here, but we can see you've done your best to tidy up and we appreciate it. We understand the mess has nothing to do with you and you seem a decent bunch of kids, so, again, thank you very much."

As we filed out, the girls took turns to hug Tina. She managed to smile once or twice and said she would see us at school.

On Monday she revealed that her parents' opinion of us

had been revised. They had found two sixth-formers enjoying a post-coital cigarette in their bed at the end of the night, oblivious to all that had gone on.

The row about fining the players rumbled on and was covered by most of the national newspapers. Gordon Taylor, chairman of the PFA, became involved.

"It smacks of the Dark Ages," he said. "I know Rochdale have financial problems but they're not cutting their wage bill at our expense."

The players took their case to the Football League Appeals Committee but Stokoe backed down on the day of the proposed hearing, revealing that they hadn't been fined after all.

"It was an attempt to motivate them. You have to explore every avenue. What I did was for the good of the club and I hope the PFA will remember that if we are all on the dole at the end of the season."

At one of my first games working with Jack a man sitting behind appeared to find my copy amusing.

"Rochdale began solidly with some neat football this afternoon..." I dictated over the phone.

"Hee, hee," from over my shoulder.

"... and Weir should have scored in the 12th minute when he headed on to the crossbar from a corner."

He was whistling now, probably to stymie the laughter. Soon afterwards my hackneyed prose caused him to tut repeatedly as if tempting a pigeon down from its perch beneath the stand.

I was only a kid learning my trade: why was he so cruel? I didn't say anything the first time it happened but readied myself for the next. He was worse than ever, not far short of one of those chuckle bags you can buy on the seafront at Blackpool. I had hardly settled in my seat when he began his impertinent giggling and whistling. He was mid-chuckle when I turned to face him. He twitched his eyebrows and made more of the sounds I had been hearing — while I was actually looking at him.

"How long until half-time?" I asked, thinking on my feet.

"About half an hour" he said, and whistled. "They've only just kicked off. What's wrong, bored already?"

Jack told me it was Les Barlow, the *Rochdale Observer*'s football correspondent whose reports I had read and filed for years. Les had a smoker's cough, a nervous tic, a frog in the throat, a maverick larynx and had been covering Rochdale so long that laughing out loud for no particular reason was permissible anyway.*

---

* I worked with Les a few years later at the *Middleton Guardian* in North Manchester where he was briefly sports editor. I never told him, of course, but it was a thrill to become friends with someone who had been so close for so long to Rochdale AFC. Despite first impressions, he remains one of the most good-natured men I've met in journalism.

After the defeat against Tranmere, Rochdale faced a long trip to free-scoring Portsmouth. The *Daily Express* journalist, Alan Thompson, accompanied them and reported back from the frontline of this 'strife-torn Fourth Division club'.

He wrote that the coach left Rochdale on Friday and the players were given packed lunches of chicken, a pickled onion, a bag of crisps, an apple and a can of pop. They stayed in a hotel overnight and, the next morning, had 'light brunch, a short walk, a team talk and set off to the match.' They lost 3–0.

On the return journey they were each given £2 which they spent on hamburgers and bangers and mash at a motorway service station. After their meal the coach wouldn't start and they pushed it across the car park to get it going. 'Didn't we have a lovely time, the day we went to Pompey,' sang the club captain, Brian Taylor. Thompson wrote: 'Laughter … and incredibly, suddenly they were men of a team again.'

The threat of fining clearly hadn't worked and probably fractured any lingering team spirit. After the Tranmere game it took them fifteen matches to record a win.

I lobbied Jack stubbornly until he agreed to take me on when I left school. The government had introduced a scheme for school leavers called the Youth Opportunities Programme. I became a *Yopper* receiving a wage of £23.50 a week from the state over a six-month period.

Most of the kids I knew were on schemes at factories or warehouses. Paul Foster was taken on at a foundry where he had to hand-paint garden gates. We met up one night and his hands were red and covered in fierce blisters; it looked as if he was wearing gloves made from bubble-wrap. The blokes at the foundry had left a hammer in the forge until it turned red. After it stopped glowing, they placed it near Paul.

"Pass us that will you?"

He said the flesh on his palm became sticky instantly. He had to lever it off using his other hand, so he had burn marks on the fingertips of his left hand too. The men laughed and told him they'd done it to stop him wanking for a few weeks.

"It's what they do," he said. "It's like testing you out. They've always done it with apprentices."

I'd recently read *The Communist Manifest,* the first few pages at least.

"You're not an apprentice though," I told him. "You're cheap labour. The history of all hitherto existing society is a history of class struggle, freeman and slave, patrician and plebeian. In a word, oppressor and oppressed ..."

I drew a table on the inside cover of one of my scrapbooks and entered our league position after every match. With the club fastened to the bottom, it began to look like a hospital heart-rate graph where the patient has fallen into a coma or died. In one sequence of results Rochdale scored just one goal in fifteen matches.

We finished at the bottom of the Football League for the second time in three seasons, eight points adrift of the next club.

Rochdale Magistrates Court became my main place of work. During weekday mornings Jack trawled the court for news stories. They were sold mainly to the *Manchester Evening News* unless there was an unusual twist that made them of interest to the nationals.

We would meet just before 10am in the press room, a windowless room containing a payphone, table and a few plastic chairs. Jack was perpetually fidgety. He patted his pockets, checked his jacket was straight, felt for his car-keys, scarf and gloves. Any minute now you felt he might dash off somewhere more interesting. He was like a young man who had fallen asleep and woken up aged sixty and was on the run from himself.

Most of the cases were trivial and barely made more than two or three paragraphs. They were petty thefts, fights in pubs, possession of drugs, people drunk on the street or scrapping with their wives and kids. The solicitors described these incidents in archaic language:

"The altercation took place after the defendant had consumed upwards of ten pints of liquor and claimed that he could vanquish anyone in the public house who would care to convene with him on the street."

Then, in an insufferably posh voice, they would revert to street language, clearly relishing the change in tack:

"At this point, the defendant said, 'You're all bastards in here, every fucking one of you. I'll take any of you on. You're a shower of shits,'."

12

On a Matter so Cataclysmic

MANY BELIEVED THAT THE FINAL HOME MATCH OF the seas on, a 2–0 defeat against Hereford United, would be our last in the Football League. The attendance of 1,318 was a couple of hundred more than usual. The extra visitors were thought to be 'ghouls,' people who called on football clubs as their death-knell sounded. They bought multiple copies of the programme and took photographs of the ground. They also availed themselves to journalists:

"We've been to all ninety-two league grounds but felt we had to come here tonight, just in case Rochdale go out," a couple from West Bromwich told the *Daily Mirror*.

Bob Stokoe was on the offensive. He censured the players —"Some of them couldn't care less about Rochdale Football Club"; the ex-manager, Doug Collins—"He said that the man who followed him into the job 'had it made.' He must have been joking"; and the fans—"It is wrong of them to blame me for something that is not of my doing."

Rochdale's position in the Football League was coveted by many, especially Altrincham, a flourishing Cheshire club who were expected to be the first to attain league status via the newly formed Alliance Premier League.

"I am quite sure that Altrincham are going to get into the League this time, so it's obvious to us what that means," said Stokoe.

The magistrates' court had a small community of regulars who were on first-name terms with the ushers. Some were from the Salvation Army hostel. Their crimes were mainly committed out of desperation, to fund addictions or because they were confused and unaware of their actions. They routinely fell asleep in the waiting room and had to be woken up.

"Come on Bob, it's your turn."

Bob would rise to his feet, startled. He usually wished the people around him a Merry Christmas (whatever time of year it was) and trailed the usher through the huge swing doors. On seeing this dishevelled figure at the back of the court, not quite sure in which direction he should head, the magistrates smiled, exchanging glances with the clerk and solicitors.

The prosecuting solicitor began:

"The man before you today is Robert William Attwood of no fixed abode. The prosecution alleges that on Saturday the eleventh of July he was drunk in the vicinity of Drake Street, Rochdale. He was seen to shout at passers-by and meander across the pavement in a way likely to obstruct pedestrians. He was, when approached by a police officer, abusive and began shouting something about cowboys and indians."

Jack knew most of the solicitors and often slipped them notes to prompt a 'line' for his story. On this occasion he wrote: 'Mention General Custer'.

The solicitor paused for a second and read the note:

"Mr Attwood had to be led away by the officer and arrested. I suppose, in the circumstances, it would be fair to say that this was Custer's last stand."

Jack had his line.

Newspapers listed the re-election dogfight as Altrincham *v* Rochdale, rather than Rochdale v Altrincham. We were the metaphorical away team, the underdogs.

Altrincham's was a persuasive case. Their average home attendance was more than 2,000 and they had spent £100,000 on their ground to accommodate these fans. They had reached the Third Round of the FA Cup three times in five seasons and their annual profit was £60,000.

They mounted an adversarial campaign, establishing Rochdale as a moth-eaten and austere concern next to their vitality and enterprise. We were old, destitute, the past, while they were new, prosperous and the future.

More so, the actual town of Rochdale represented a bygone era, of mills and manual work, a blue collar anachronism sunk deep into the Lancashire heartland. Altrincham was part of affluent Cheshire, a place where the business class of Manchester returned at the end of the working day.

Jack didn't have enough work to keep me occupied so when he went on holiday he said I could take a month off. I found a temporary job at a book wholesaler, GW Johnson's, based in a dingy building on the outskirts of the town centre.

The place had a distinctive smell of damp, paper and fumes from the calor gas fires. I'd push my bike into the storeroom and report to Bill, the foreman. He was usually pressed close to the fire, his thin grey coat lifted at the back so the heat could get to his backside. He was small and wiry, at least 60-years-old, and completely bald apart from a snake of grey hair that ran from ear to ear above his neck. He was bow-legged but remarkably agile and strong. He had what my dad called 'laughing eyes' and you were never sure where he was looking. He'd start talking and I'd not realise he was speaking to me.

"Sorry Bill."

"Are-you-with-us-this-morning?" he'd ask slowly.

I had to make the first brew of the day for the four or five people that worked there. After I had handed everyone their cups on the second day, I was told to 'listen up'.

"You're not a reckless lad are you?"

"No, Bill."

"Good. I don't want you messing with these cups, see."

"I won't."

"Good."

"Why?"

"There was a serious accident here once involving a cup."

My mouth fell open.

"What happened?"

"Someone nearly lost an eye, that's what."

About ten years earlier a lad called Phil had drunk his tea and mimed that he was going to throw the dregs into someone's face. The cup flew off its handle and hit one of the reps above the eye. He needed stitches and was off work for a few days.

"You see," said Bill. "Accidents can happen at work, just like that."

He clicked his fingers as he said 'just like that.'

Fred Ratcliffe, now club president, faithfully sent out letters to the chairmen of the other ninety-one clubs. He was probably aware that he was conducting a poll of his own popularity. The chairmen of first and second division clubs held most votes but these seldom played Rochdale or were particularly concerned about them. If, however, they had met *Little Freddie* or, as he was often termed, *Mr Rochdale*, and remembered him, they might lend their support. On a matter so cataclysmic as ending a football club's League tenure it was easier to transmute the issue to a sentimental basis.

"It will be the most shattering day of my life if we are thrown out," Ratcliffe told reporters.

Did they really want to break Fred's heart?

Bill was a hard worker and mesmeric with a piece of string, a pile of books and a Stanley knife. He knew the location of every book and file in a warehouse containing thousands of them. He could tell the sound of a *Rippo* van's engine [Ripponden Carriers] through a brick wall lined with hundreds of boxes. He was so keyed into the company's business—the arrival of deliveries, phone calls from reps—that he knew the time at all points of the day without looking at his watch.

I hadn't realised that most of the book trade was devoted to romances and westerns. We stacked box after box of these, along with colouring books, comics and puzzle magazines ready to be taken to markets throughout the north.

Sheila was one of the reps. She was in her late thirties and a slim, attractive woman. She had red hair that fell down her face in tight ringlets. When she called in, the mood lifted behind her trail of perfume.

"Hello Sheila, my love," sang Bill.

He whistled as well and set about his tasks with even more relish and efficiency. She fell coy around his quaint flirting. After she'd gone he imagined I'd found her irresistible.

"That's a proper woman, that is. A classy piece. Don't even think about tapping her up. She'd have you for bloody breakfast."

Most of the stock was kept downstairs. The first floor was practically derelict with broken windows and missing floorboards. Pigeons flew around the eaves and small mounds of dust formed beneath slates that had worked loose. Buckets were dotted around to catch the rain. The toilet was in the corner, a cold, windowless room formed from a mismatch of chipboard and plywood.

An hour or two after Sheila had left, I went in there. Bill

was waiting for me at the bottom of the stairs.

"Hey, you've not been pulling it up there have you?" he shouted.

As I passed he pretended to cuff me around the back of the head:

"Don't be having any lurid thoughts about Sheila now."

The annual meeting of the Football League was set for Friday 6 June, 1980 at the Café Royal in London. The voting for re-election was due to take place at around 2.30 pm.

Bill's assistant was Alfie, a big bloke in his early thirties who still lived at home with his mother. Bill teased him that he was still a virgin. Alfie played along but after a while it was obvious the subject made him uncomfortable.

"Are we going to do any work today or what?" he'd ask.

Alfie drifted upstairs most lunchtimes to sit with the pigeons and eat sandwiches his mum had made for him. I followed on and we sat down on upturned crates, facing each other. He looked despondent. I asked what was wrong.

"It's Bill, he pisses me off sometimes."

I'd heard them talking that morning. Bill had been badgering Alfie, saying he was tied to his mum's apron strings and he'd never get a girlfriend while he spent so much time with her. She was running his life for him. Couldn't she do her own shopping? And why did he give up his Friday nights ferrying her to and from the Bingo like a glorified taxi driver? He should live his own life. He wasn't a kid anymore.

Alfie thought he was put-upon at work too. He wasn't employed as a driver but was constantly being asked to deliver books in the van. He told me his wage and asked if I thought it was enough for what he did. His hourly rate was only a few pence more than I was being paid. I asked if he was in a union.

"You're joking. They wouldn't have the union in here. They'd shut the place down."

I told him to get some proper advice. He became tetchy. He rose to his feet and screwed up the paper his butties had been wrapped in. I thought he was going to throw it but he put it in his trouser pocket.

"What does it matter to you anyway? You'll bugger off to college or something won't you? I'll still be here when you've long gone."

The next day while Alfie was taking the mail to the Post Office, Bill asked for a 'quiet word'. He rubbed his hands on his coat and twitched his eyebrows:

"Look, I don't know exactly what you've been saying to Alfie but it might not be a good idea to say any more. I think you upset him yesterday. He's a sensitive lad you know, it doesn't take much to set him off."

We were on our afternoon tea break when news came through about the re-election vote at the Café Royal. The radio was on and it was the last item of the bulletin; the announcer had said earlier that he had 'important news coming up for fans of Altrincham and Rochdale who were desperate to hear about their club's future.'

I was sitting away from the others on a ledge by the doorway to the first floor. The sun was filtering through the windows and I could see particles of dust floating languidly across the room.

He broke the news: Rochdale had been voted back into the Football League by one vote. I leaned back and closed my eyes, almost swooning. I felt a rush of relief and happiness and love and joy. I tried to tell Bill and Alfie how important it was but they didn't understand.

"They're rubbish anyway. I don't know why anyone's bothered about them."

Bill, noting my exhilaration, said this probably meant I wouldn't mind nipping to the shop, buying some Kit Kats and brewing up for everyone when I got back. As I skipped through the front door, he shouted:

"And don't piss yourself in all your excitement."

Bob Stokoe left the club, telling newspapers, 'the job's too big for me.' He was photographed marching defiantly away, holdall in hand. He wore a light cardigan over a Polo shirt, his bald pate covered by strands of hair neatly trained from the side of his head. He looked like a man suddenly free of anxiety, a man on his way to the airport or the train station, a man who had served his time and suffered enough. He said he had delayed his resignation because he didn't want to harm the club's re-election bid.

The message implicit in Rochdale's fortuitous re-election* was that the club had been granted one last chance. If they did not evade the bottom four during the forthcoming season, they would be expelled.

---

* It was, in fact, even more fortuitous than first thought. Two club chairmen travelling to the meeting together were involved in a car accident and missed the ballot. Apparently they had both planned to vote for Altrincham's election to the League. By rights the exact location of this accident should be marked with a plaque stating that it is the re-birthplace of Rochdale Association Football Club. Great story though this is, another version has it that the Luton Town chairman was stuck in a traffic jam and his Grimsby Town counterpart messed up his voting paper. Both refused to reveal who would have been the recipient of their votes. The plaque will have to wait.

13

A Chuckle in his Boots

WHENEVER I WAS ILL I THUMBED THROUGH MY collection of Rochdale programmes; it was therapeutic. I had copies dating back to the late-1940s. The pages were turning yellow. Team-changes and scorers were scrawled in blotchy ink on the back pages. The players had peculiar hairstyles — short, long, high fringes, sideburns, crew cuts, side-partings, and they had names like Ted, Duggie, Ray, Bert, Harold, Geo and Eric.

On the photographs you could see the familiar scenery — the trees peering above the stand at the Sandy Lane end; the grass on 'the hill'; the stands; the terraces. The players, smiling with arms folded, were passing through but the background remained. They were like members of a family, your older brothers or your uncles perhaps, photographed in the same house where you now lived but long before you were even born. When you held the programmes you were a late-arrival at these games, a figure slipping over the turnstiles from thirty years in the future, lost in the crowd, brushing the rain from your lapels.

Until I began working for Jack I hadn't given any thought to how programmes came to exist. I imbued their production with magic and romance, as I did with much of a football club's business. I didn't envisage them being written by anyone or printed but merely appearing on the day of a match, much as the team did three minutes before kick-off.

When Jack agreed that I could contribute to the programme I was incredulous that I would form part of this sorcery and immortality. Some kid, thirty years from now, might see my name in there, read my words, and ponder (as I did): if he were fifteen-years-old when he wrote this piece, he would now be forty-five. What had happened to him? Did he still support the club? Did he marry? Did he move from the area? Did he have children? Did he still look anything like he did then?*

Peter Madden, a 42-year-old ex-guardsman, was made manager after serving as an assistant to both Doug Collins and Bob Stokoe. He was a giant, taking up the space of two men when he stood, shoulders back, arms by his side, on official team photographs.

His first task was to refute allegations that Rochdale were on the verge of folding.

---

* The irony of this has not passed me by. It is almost thirty years since I contributed to the programme. Ouch.

"There is no question of us not starting the new season in the Football League. Rochdale has a long history of League football and we are not going to lose that," he said.

His players were going to work so hard that they 'singed the grass' and he revealed:

"This is more than a job to me. It is a cause. I am sure that I will be able to motivate the players again."

The first signing was Eugene Martinez. Although born in Chelmsford, we soon discovered that he was loyal to the stereotype of his Latin ancestry. Roguishly handsome, he was a skilful winger with an array of tricks, jigs, pullbacks and side steps. If Rochdale were winning and he had the better of the full back, you could almost hear the chuckle in his boots as he sashayed to the by-line. If Rochdale were toiling, however, and their full back proving implacable, Martinez brooded. He'd take a dig in the defender's ribs or arrive late with a tackle. Finally, if his opponent continued to mark him tight and was reckless with his challenges, Martinez sought retribution. Thud. Goodnight. The little winger would make his way to the changing rooms, waving his arms, arguing with no one in particular, pushing away team-mates. The referee had no need to formally send him off; Martinez was already on the team coach, telling the driver how the whole world was against him and no one understood him, ever.

The programme, much like the club, was in a sorry state. It was printed on the cheapest paper, usually without pictures or colour, and with little thought given to design or content. Supporters were able to read it in minutes and copies were often discarded afterwards, jammed between seats or tossed aside on the terraces.

It was a make-do affair; sketchy and full of mistakes, proof that no one really cared. Jack had taken over the editorship on a voluntary basis because there was no one else to do it. Without Jack's input, the club might have been forced to issue team-sheets.

The copy swarmed with spelling mistakes, almost one on every line. Players' names were habitually spelled wrong, including Rochdale's. Jimmy Seal was Jimmy Seel for most of the season, while there were obvious misgivings about opponents supposedly called Leville Southall, Dave Beaufant, Elvin Edwards, Franny Fur, Wayne Wankly and Dreak Hampton.

The articles read as if supplied by someone still learning the rudiments of the English language. David Esser was profiled in the programme for the match against Hartlepool United. It began: 'Young Dave Esser may not be happy about it, but we don't really know but most Rochdale fans are happy that Dave, who wanted a move towards the end of last season, is still with us, in a regular First team place and producing the goods more effectively than ever.' It closed: 'He is interested in most sports and if there is one thing he likes less than losing a match it is the decimation of the world's whales.'

The quarter-page devoted to the visitors contained pro-saic homilies like, "Rochdale fans welcome their visitors [Bury] from their next door neighbours and hope for an entertaining match to which we are sure our visitors are capable of making a fair contribution.'

I began by writing a page called *News at Four*. I read through daily and local papers and gleaned information about other clubs in our division. I was surprised when Jack asked me if I also wanted to write Peter Madden's page.

"Doesn't do it himself?"

"Does he buggery. He's too busy."

"What shall I write?"

"Anything you want as long as it's not daft and you don't single out one of the players for a slagging off."

A few weeks later I became the voice of Peter Madden. I adopted Jack's technique of issuing banalities about the lads needing to pull up their socks or knuckle down and stay focused for the month ahead.

The signing of Barry Wellings from York City completed the forward line. Wellings — and even the *Rochdale Observer* noted this — was 'golden haired'. Indeed, he had the kind of long velvety, flaxen hair worn by heroines in the Ladybird well-loved tales series we'd all read as kids. If his hair was Cinderella, his short, bulky physique and pointy chin was a troll set free and dressed in a football kit.

Also coming to the fore was a young striker called Mark Hilditch, known universally as *Spoonface* such was the uniqueness of his facial features.

Peter Madden assembled his squad of side-show evacuees at the pre-season photo call. This time, in their matching tops and shorts, they at least appeared to be of the same

Peter Madden, definitely not pretending to make a phone call.

gang. The picture showed them performing sit-ups on a piece of land that looked like wasteground between the chip shop and the launderette on the nearest council estate—the fence ripped down behind them, clumps of uncut grass. These were the men and the facilities from which the future of Rochdale AFC would have to be forged.

Dad drove me across town with my typed sheets of copy ready for the printers. The entrance was down a narrow alleyway covered in dog muck and crushed cans of beer. A tiny sign identified that it was a printers. I knocked. No answer. I knocked again, harder. No one came. I felt for the door handle and pushed it down.

It was dark inside. The machines roared, spewing out reams of paper. The air was heavy with the acrid smell of ink. I saw a few Rochdale programmes lying around. Those left out on benches were covered in circle stains from mugs. Some were loose on the floor, torn and scuffed, footprints across them.

The man closest to the door was collating paper. He glanced when I entered but looked away and carried on working. I waved my hand. He pretended not to notice, turning his back to me as he started another pile. I walked over and stood a few feet away from him.

"I've got some stuff for the Rochdale programme," I mouthed.

He shook his head.

"I've got some stuff for the Rochdale programme."

He nodded as if he understood then moved his head to the side. He was gesturing that I had to see someone else on the other side of the room. I walked down a small passageway between two machines and saw an older man holding down a lever. He had ink on his forehead. He held up his free hand as I approached. After a few seconds he pulled back the lever and shouted.

"What do you want?"

"I've got some stuff for the Rochdale programme."

"You're a bit late, aren't you?"

"Jack said if I got it to you a week before the match you could use it."

"Who's this bloody Jack fella?"

"Jack Hammill, he edits the programme."

"Well I've not bloody met him. It's turning into a right fucking job this is."

I shrugged my shoulders.

"We've got that pillock from the supporters' club coming in with his bits of paper, Jack fucking what's-is-name and now you. Why can't we have the lot in one go? You can't run a magazine like this, in dribs and drabs."

I said I was only doing as I was asked. He softened slightly.

"We've nearly finished setting the pages for the next one. We'll have to make another plate now."

He put the pieces of paper containing my articles on a table overflowing with notes. I said what I was thinking:

"You won't lose it will you?"

"No, I won't fucking lose it," he barked, picking up an empty mug and slamming it down.

I left them to set the copy in metal. They must have undertaken the job after a visit to the pub because most of the punctuation was omitted, strange words appeared randomly and lines sloped up or down.

I was bitterly upset the first few times my by-line was left out; after a few weeks I began to think it was for the best.

During the summer of 1980 a rusty horseshoe was unearthed at Spotland that was thought to have belonged to Dolly, a horse that had pulled a roller across the turf fifty years earlier. It was nailed to the door of the home changing room and in their first six games Rochdale lost just once, moving to the fringes of the promotion zone. It was their best start to a season since 1925.

I had more or less packed in playing football after the experiences with Nigel O'Loughlin and Mr Smithies. I had also suffered a couple of injuries, including a gashed knee that kept me out for months.

Farrel Bridge FC were struggling to find enough players to put out a team. They were near the bottom of the last division in the Rochdale Amateur League. Their manager, one of the engineers at the factory where the team was based, asked my dad if I'd like to play for them. I was fifteen and small for my age so they put me on the wing.

"You won't get kicked in the air as much out there."

We lost the first game I played but in the second we unexpectedly beat the league leaders 3–0. Two or three others had joined at the same time and we immediately read each other's game and played well together. The other players were much older than me and extremely competitive. If I was playing well and beating the full back, they encouraged me to 'take the piss.' Defenders didn't like this and chopped me down; I could usually jump over their shins. My team-mates would steam in two yards behind, pushing the defender in the chest, telling him to get a fucking life and leave the kid alone. Some spent the entire match talking and shouting. The referees swore back:

"I'm the ref here. Piss off if you don't like it."

Matches were played out against this backdrop of bickering and spleen, players squaring up and pushing one another in the back. They threw punches; not the comedy punches of the professional game but cold, crisp whacks against the side of the face.

We played at Buckley Hall, the local detention centre, and their team included three or four black lads. I'd never heard so many names for a black person before. I was told to mark the egg and spoon [coon], get tight to the cat and dog [wog] and keep a look out for the bunny [jungle bunny]. After the game both teams shook hands warmly and patted each other on the back: it had all been in the name of sport, apparently.

Barry Wellings scored once in his first thirteen league matches but as the pitches became sodden in the autumn, he was a revelation. He adapted his game to his physique. Since he had no legs to speak of, he had greater mobility

Match of the (grey) Day: Farrel Bridge v Torchbearers,
Firgrove, Rochdale.

sliding across the turf on his backside. A malaise in the opponents' penalty area would end abruptly with the unexpected arrival of Wellings. A golden glow flashed across the grass, ball and backside collided and the ball usually hit the net. Wellings would jump to his feet triumphantly and acknowledge the goal, levering a good portion of the Spotland pitch from the back of his shorts as he made his way to the half-way line.

In between the feuds and fighting Farrel Bridge played some good football and the winning streak lifted the team to mid-table. The company was pleased and bought us medals and held an end-of-season presentation night.

My dad sometimes drank in a pub close to the engineering works and overheard a conversation while he was at the bar. Two blokes were talking about Farrel Bridge's upturn in form.

"Apparently they've signed some kid who plays on the wing and he's been waltzing past everyone."

When, the next day, he told me what he'd heard I had the impression that little else I might achieve in life would surpass the feeling of happiness and well-being caused by overhearing that snippet of conversation.

At the presentation night we arranged to reconvene in July for pre-season training. Before then the works introduced a programme of redundancies. Many lost their jobs and the team was disbanded.

Peter Madden's commitment to enterprising football and his dynamism ("These players will die for me") galvanised the club. Fans rallied. Members of the supporters' club trudged around the pitch at most home matches carrying a blanket into which fans tossed coins. Some shuffled down the terraces to place them in but others saw this as their half-time entertainment. They hurled the money through the air and a cheer broke out whenever someone was hit on the back of the head. If their aim was true, an official fell to his knees and the blanket tipped-up at one corner. Money cascaded on to the pitch: jackpot! The other blanket-carriers shouted into the stands:

"Will you give over? You'll have someone's bloody eye out."

Volunteers painted the ground on Sundays. Rochdale Karate Club raised £100 with a sponsored press-ups session. Mr Greaves, an 84-year-old from Coventry, promised the club £1 for every win—half of his weekly spending money. A group of fans collected money in a dustbin they pushed around the town centre, led by a Labrador wearing a royal blue ribbon. The directors' wives held potato pie suppers. One supporter, Tony Lord, donated £125 of his own money.

These were, in themselves, small measures but they formed a sense of community that had long been missing. The Dale were on the up.

I continually made errors while covering matches at Rochdale. At one game Jack reiterated on numerous occasions that I shouldn't forget to put the final score across to the BBC. He told me so many times he made me nervous. With four or five minutes remaining I rang them with the 'final' score. Jack overheard and began shouting:

"What have you just done? What have you just done?"

"I've given the score to the BBC."

"But the bloody game's not finished you half-wit"

Until this point what I had done seemed perfectly logical. In fact, I congratulated myself on my efficiency. I'd got the job done with time to spare.

Jack was in mid-flow dictating copy when he apprehended me. He still had the phone in his hand. A scratchy voice was repeating at the other end:

"Hello, Jack, Jack … are you there?"

Jack was somewhere else, no longer of this earth.

"You fucking ring them up. Do you hear me? The game's not over yet. If someone scores now, we've had it. Ring them up."

He was waving the phone around and I thought he might club me with it.* While I was trying to get through to the BBC, the referee blew the whistle to end the game. Jack looked across, sighing and shaking his head.

"I'm going to have to bloody watch you."

---

* Another time I saw Jack livid was when we were discussing *Rap's* revelations about Fred Ratcliffe. "Fancy following an old man around like that," he said. "Little Freddie deserves more respect for what he's done for this town and the football club. They're just… [he stopped for a second to think of the right words, then spat out] sneaky bastards. That's all they are, sneaky bastards."

And he did watch me, and listen too. He picked me up on my grammar. At one game, during which he had corrected my English several times, I joined his mood of despairing on my behalf.

"Why am I so unaccurate Jack?"

His heart skipped a beat. Or maybe *un*skipped one.

"Unaccurate? Unaccurate? You can't help yourself, can you? You've just done it again. There's no such word. Do you mean inaccurate?"*

Rochdale maintained their good form and were two points from a promotion place in mid-January. Madden agreed they had a chance of escaping the bottom division via the unexpected route of going up, not down.

"Yes, it could possibly happen for us now," he said.

The club immediately set upon its worst run of the season, recording one win in the next ten matches. The season closed on a relatively disappointing note with Rochdale in 15th place but still seven points clear of the re-election

---

* The experience of working with Jack was invaluable, an authentic 'old school' training but after the YOP ended I decided on a formal route. I was accepted on a full-time college course in journalism. I lost touch afterwards and only spoke to him properly on one more occasion. I was disgruntled, feeling under-valued and over-worked on an evening newspaper. I phoned and asked whether he thought it was a good idea to turn freelance, as he had done years before. He unequivocally and determinedly warned me against it. "Stay put," he said. All these years on, I still consider it the worst advice I have ever been given, though, of course, it was well-meant.

zone. Bob Stokoe had said earlier it would be a 'miracle' if Rochdale avoided the bottom four.

In the final match programme of the season Wyn Rawlinson, the club secretary, published a poem dedicated to the team built by Madden. She said the second verse fitted 'quite well' to the tune of *John Brown's Body* and fans were asked to sing it on the terraces:

'And Peter Madden's mercenaries are hot on the trail,
They have got the courage and the spirit to do well,
Though the road be long their all-out effort will not fail,
As they go marching on.'

No one sang it, of course. Instead they did as they had always done, and still do today: a long moan of 'Daaaaaaayyyyyuuuul.'

POMONA BOOKS

POMONA IS A WHOLLY INDEPENDENT PUBLISHER DEDICATED to bringing before the public the work of prodigiously talented writers. Tell your friends. Our books can be purchased on-line at:

www.pomonauk.com

A free Pomona Sounds CD will be sent with every order.

ALSO AVAILABLE:

F O O T N O T E * by Boff Whalley
ISBN 1-904590-00-4 · £8.99

FOOTNOTE IS CLEVER, FUNNY AND IRREVERENT — A STORY ABOUT A boy from the redbrick clichés of smalltown England reconciling Mormonism and punk rock, industrial courtesy and political insurrection.

He finds a guitar, anarchism and art terrorism and, after years (and years and years) of earnest, determined, honest-to-goodness slogging, his pop group† makes it big; that's BIG with a megaphone actually. They write a song that has the whole world singing and, funnily enough, it's an admirable summary of a life well lived — about getting knocked down and getting back up again.

Meanwhile, there's a whole world still happening: authentic lives carefully drawn, emotional but not sentimental and always with a writer's eye for detail. *Footnote* is not another plodding rock memoir but a compassionate, critical and sometimes cynical account of a life steeped in pop culture, lower division football and putting the world to rights.

---

* See page 293 of Boff Whalley's book.

† Boff Whalley is a member of Chumbawamba.

RULE OF NIGHT by Trevor Hoyle
ISBN 1-904590-01-2 · £8.99

IF THE SIXTIES WERE SWINGING, THE SEVENTIES WERE THE HANG-
over — darker, nastier, uglier — especially if you lived on a council estate in
the north of England.

Rule of Night was first published in 1975 and has since become a cult classic. It pre-dates the current vogue for 'hard men' and 'football hoolie' books
by 25 years.

It is, however, much more than this. Trevor Hoyle creates a chillingly
detailed world, where teenagers prowl rainy fluorescent-lit streets dressed
as their *Clockwork Orange* anti-heroes. The backdrop is provided by Ford
Cortinas, Players No.6, the factory, the relentless struggle to maintain hope.

Hoyle, who has since been published by John Calder (home to Samuel
Beckett and William S. Burroughs), has added a fascinating afterword to his
original book which has been out of print and highly sought-after for many
years.

. . .

THE FAN by Hunter Davies
ISBN 1-904590-02-0 · £9.99

HUNTER DAVIES IS ONE OF BRITAIN'S MOST ACCLAIMED WRITERS
and journalists. He has written over 30 books, among them modern classics,
The Beatles and *A Walk Around The Lakes*. *The Glory Game*, published in
1972, is a benchmark work on football and is still in print today.

The Fan is a collection of very personal, unusual pieces about his life as a
supporter. He observes football in its sovereignty of the late 1900s and early
2000s and tackles the big topics of the day: Beckham's haircuts, high finance,
the price of pies, the size of match day programmes, the enormous wages,
the influence of Sky TV, England's numerous managers.

Along the way, he also lets us into his home life, in London and the Lake
District, his family, his work, his tortoise, his poorly knee (caused by too
much Sunday football).

Originally published in the *New Statesman* magazine, *The Fan* catches
Davies at his very best and most amusing. It will appeal to supporters of any
age, sex and loyalties.

LOVE SONGS by Crass

ISBN 1-904590-03-9 · £9.99

> *Our love of life is total,*
> *everything we do is an expression of that.*
> *Everything that we write is a love song.*
> – Penny Rimbaud, *Yes, Sir, I Will*

CRASS: A RURAL COLLECTIVE BASED IN ESSEX, FORMED IN 1977 OF A diverse and eclectic group of individuals who operated for several years using music, art, literature and film as vehicles to share information and ideas. They also wanted to change the world.

This is a collection of words spanning those seven short years; a book of shock slogans and mindless token tantrums. An anthology of passionate love songs that sought to inspire a generation, and succeeded.

. . .

SUM TOTAL by Ray Gosling

ISBN 1-904590-05-5 · £9.99

SUM TOTAL IS A LOST MASTERPIECE OF BRITISH LITERATURE, a restless, hungry riposte to America's finest Beat writers.

Written in 1961 when he was just 21, Gosling's itchy 'sort of' autobiography is a startlingly original take on the England of the early Sixties: rock 'n' roll, trains, dead-end jobs, drizzle, hitchhiking, jukebox cafés, trudging through hometown streets.

All the time he remains gloriously indulgent, disillusioned yet hopeful, tired but desperate for every new day.

Although now famous for hundreds of television and radio documentaries, in *Sum Total* Gosling reveals himself as a writer years ahead of his time, presenting a skew-whiff, arch and droll view of the world, both inside and out.

He has added a typically idiosyncratic and lengthy preface to the original text.

DIARY OF A HYPERDREAMER
by Bill Nelson
ISBN 1-904590-06-3 · £9.99

BILL NELSON IS ONE OF BRITAIN'S MOST RESPECTED CREATIVE forces. He came to prominence in the Seventies with Be Bop Deluxe and later Red Noise. He has collaborated with like-minds such as Yellow Magic Orchestra, David Sylvian, Harold Budd and Roger Eno and still releases a prolific amount of new music.

Diary of a Hyperdreamer is his day-by-day journal in which he ponders on life, art and the nation. His unique perspective is fed by a career creating and producing music, photography, painting and video.

Written from his home in a hamlet in north Yorkshire, he also includes engaging details of his family life, regular musings on mortality, along with reflections on his childhood and former life as a globe-trotting 'pop star.'

. . .

THE PRICE OF COAL by Barry Hines
ISBN 1-904590-08-x · £9.99

BARRY HINES IS A MASTER CRAFTSMAN. WHILE HE IS RIGHTLY celebrated for his classic, *A Kestrel for a Knave* (later filmed as *Kes*), his other work is equally powerful.

The Price of Coal is an uncompromising depiction of life at a colliery where beer, snooker, cricket and time spent on the allotment is the only respite from clawing coal from the earth.

A royal visit prompts the introduction of soft soap to the toilets, grass seeds scattered on the slag heap, and lashings of white paint across the site.

But when disaster strikes the superficial is forgotten as men fight for their lives in the darkness underneath collapsing seams of coal.

As ever, Hines proves himself an exemplary storyteller with a discerning eye for detail and when bolder, gaudier writing is long forgotten, his stays in the mind and nourishes it.

He has written a new foreword to the original text which was first published in 1979 and later adapted for television as two linked plays, directed by Ken Loach in the acclaimed *Play for Today* series.

L O O K S & S M I L E S by Barry Hines

ISBN 1-904590-09-8 · £9.99

LOOKS AND SMILES IS A LOST BULLETIN FROM THE EARLY-EIIGHTIES when the sun felt to have set permanently on hope and optimism. Unemployment was rampant, especially in the north where traditional industries were laid waste by Margaret Thatcher and her government.

Set amid this gloom, *Looks and Smiles* is an under-stated love affair between unemployed school-leaver Mick and Karen who works in a town centre shoe shop. They both want little more from life than a decent chance.

As ever, Hines proves himself an exemplary storyteller with a discerning eye for detail. He never resorts to sentimentality, and hope, however slender, flickers always.

The book was originally published in 1981 and later made into a film by Ken Loach.

. . .

K I C K E D I N T O T O U C H (PLUS EXTRA-TIME) by Fred Eyre

ISBN 1-904590-12-8 · £9.99

FRED EYRE'S SPORTING LIFE BEGAN FULL OF PROMISE WHEN he became Manchester City's first ever apprentice. He never made their first team. In fact, he seldom made anyone's first team. Injuries played a part but limited talent was the greater curse. As he plummeted down the leagues he had something few footballers possess: a stud-sharp memory and an ability to write humorously about the sport he loves.

Originally published in 1981, *Kicked Into Touch* has become an enigma — selling more than a million copies yet still retaining cult status within the sport and among fans. This new version has been completely revised, extended and updated with a new set of photographs included.

It is set to reach a new generation of football fans looking for an antidote to the glib reportage of a sport lost to show business.

MEAN WITH MONEY by Hunter Davies
ISBN 1-904590-13-6 · £9.99

AT LAST, A BOOK ABOUT MONEY THAT TELLS IT STRAIGHT: PUT IT under the bed. All of it. Sure, it makes for easy access to burglars but better them than the felons passing themselves off as financial advisors or acting as foot-soldiers for organisations with words like union, mutual, trust, alliance, equitable or assurance in their name.

Mean With Money, inspired by Hunter Davies' well-loved column in *The Sunday Times*, is wilfully short on practical advice but offers instead good humour and much-needed empathy as we face the corporate horror of high-handed and indifferent financial institutions.

Davies, one of Britain's most celebrated writers, also looks at ingenious ways to save money (cut your own hair, for starters) and what to do with it when it arrives. Along the way, he reveals details of his regular visits to McDonald's (it's free to use their toilets), the eccentric old ladies who staff his local Oxfam shop and the swim that cost him £333.

Famous for seminal works on The Beatles, football, and subjects as diverse as lottery winners and walking disused railway tracks, Davies is, once more, on top form. Go get 'em Hunt.

. . .

ZONE OF THE INTERIOR by Clancy Sigal
ISBN 1-904590-10-1 · £9.99

'THE BOOK THEY DARED NOT PRINT', ZONE OF THE INTERIOR IS a lost classic of zonked-out, high-as-a-kite Sixties literature. It tells the story of Sid Bell, an American political fugitive in London, who falls under the spell of Dr. Willie Last (partly modelled on the radical 'anti-psychiatrist' RD Laing). This unlikely duo feast on LSD, mescaline, psilocybin and psycho-babble, believing that only by self-injecting themselves with schizo-phrenia will they become true existentialist guerrillas. Their 'purple haze' odyssey takes them into the eye of the hurricane — mental hospitals, secure units for the violent, the Harley Street cabal of the 'Sacred 7' and semi-derelict churches that come complete with an underground tank for the woman convinced she's a fish. Sigal's approach is richly sardonic and anti-establishment, of both right and left, in a jazz-influenced free-form prose, comic and serious, myth-puncturing and elegiac. Along the way Sigal, now an established Hollywood screen-writer, makes the case for a revolutionary period of mental health nursing whose task is as yet undone.

THE ARMS OF THE INFINITE
by Christopher Barker

ISBN 1-904590-04-7 · £9.99

CHRISTOPHER BARKER IS THE SON OF THE CULT WRITER ELIZABETH Smart (*By Grand Central Station I Sat Down and Wept*) and the notorious poet, George Barker.

The Arms of the Infinite takes the reader inside the minds of both parents and, from their first fateful meeting and subsequent elopement, Barker candidly reveals their obsessive, passionate and volatile love affair.

He writes evocatively of his unconventional upbringing with his siblings in a shack in Ireland and, later, a rambling, falling-down house in Essex. Interesting and charismatic figures from the literary and art worlds are regular visitors and the book is full of fascinating cameos and anecdotes.

Barker is himself a gifted writer. An early draft of his memoir formed a cover story for the literary magazine, *Granta*.

. . .

THE SECOND HALF
ISBN 1-904590-14-4 · £9.99

SING IT LOUD: THERE'S ONLY ONE HUNTER DAVIES, ONE HUNTER DAVIES. And he's still, in all fairness Brian, bang on top form, doing well, the lad.

The Second Half is another collection of his personal pieces from the *New Statesman* covering the past three domestic seasons; the Euro Championship of 2004; and the 2006 World Cup when he unexpectedly became Wayne Rooney's top buddy.

'When a player gets sent off shouldn't we fans get some of our money back?' ponders Davies in one piece. 'I just wish he'd shave his stupid face,' he berates José Mourhino in another. And, goooaaal!, Hunt rumbles Sven early doors: 'He's a spare swede at a veggie gathering. What is the point of him?' he writes two years before England's World Cup debacle.

As ever, his outlook is fiercely that of the fan — disgruntled, bewildered and passionate — wondering what the players do with all that money, all those girls, and why match programmes are 'full of adverts or arse-licks for sponsors.'

He comically portrays his on-off relationship with young Rooney, from cheerily declaring that he 'likes his ugliness' to becoming his official biographer after coming first in a beauty competition (just like in Monopoly).

And, finally, why did Peter Crouch? Because he saw Darren Bent, of course.

There's more to life than books you know,
but not much more ...

POMONA SOUNDS

POMONA SOUNDS IS OUR AFFILIATED RECORD LABEL.
The following CD albums are available on-line at :

www.pomonauk.com:

PS-001	The Rosenbergs *Ameripop*	£7
PS-002	Black September *Black September*	£10
PS-003	Mudskipper *Eggshells*	£10
PS-004	The Monkey Run *Escape From The Rake*	£10
PS-005	Crass *You'll Ruin It For Everyone*	£10
PS-006	Killing Stars *When The Light First Fell*	£10
PS-007	Black September *You Can Do Anything*	
	If You Set Your Mind To It	£10

. . .